Roe on the Go

A Senior's Travel Reflections

Rosemary Lamour

PublishAmerica
Baltimore

First printing

ISBN: 1-4241-5573-8
PUBLISHED BY PUBLISHAMERICA, LLLP
www.publishamerica.com
Baltimore

Printed in the United States of America

PROLOGUE

My dear lovely, handsome, talented grandchildren:
Jennifer, Aislynn, Philip, Michael, Bradley, Kjersten,
Gregory, Alex, Will, Kelsey, Heidi, Emma
&
My darling great-grandchildren:
Elysabeth, Collin, Danielle, Cooper

This book is for you!

I am putting together this account of my journeys to inspire
you to travel around this wonderful world God has given us.

You, no doubt, have seen pictures of the world as viewed
from a space shuttle. It appears as a little ball, the size of a
grapefruit, seemingly suspended in nothingness. We are each
one granule on its surface for a short period in time.

So many travel books have been written. Some stress the
educational value, the pictorial worth, the language and
customs of each country and its people—whatever is the
agenda of the author.

I like to think the beauty of this world touches our soul, if we
let it. It is a gem to treasure for our lifetimes, to ponder the
mysteries of heaven and its Creator. The people whom you will
meet are doing the best with what they have in the environment

God has placed them. They will open their hearts to you, if you but go with a smile on your face and in your heart. Travel without arrogance—humbly and simply.

And so I want to tell you briefly about my trips to Italy, Ireland, London, Central Europe, Scotland, England, and finally to Alaska. All of these trips took place between 1996 and 2003, in my late seventies, on a limited budget. Not in my wildest dreams did I ever expect to spend my retirement years in such a fashion! You can do the same. But when you are young, can backpack, stay at youth hostels, take sport trips, and tackle difficult terrain, many new dimensions are added to the world of travel. I would encourage you, at any age, to rent a car and travel with your loved one through back roads and country towns, staying at B & Bs along the way. It's a great way to know the country and people you are visiting.

I have prefaced my account of each country with copies of letters I sent to your parents and aunts and uncles after each return. I wrote, not with the purpose of describing every site and every incident in detail, but rather a wish to convey my impressions of what I experienced. Re-reading them, I realize there are some gaps where I took for granted my readers would know what I was referencing. Now, I want to fill in these empty places with some descriptions for my younger readers.

I was most blessed in having my niece, Eileen, accompany me on every trip, except for Italy. Eileen is a first-grade teacher in Pueblo, Colorado, and half my age. We traveled on organized tours with strangers from around the world. Eileen and I gave each other space to do our own thing. For example, Eileen was a shop-a-holic. (It is a trying experience for me to even go into shopping centers.) She covered almost every boutique in Ireland with a fellow tour member from the midwest, while I lounged with other travelers back at the hotel.

Hold on to your hats—we are off to Italy.

With all my love,

MEME

July 17, 2003
(My 81st birthday!)

ITALY
September 23–October 2, 1996

Dear Family & Friends,

I returned home from Italy on Wednesday at 10:30 a.m. (4:30 a.m. Rome time). We had been up for over twenty-three hours! Our flight time from Miami to Rome was eleven hours; on return, we detoured to Milan which added two hours to the trip. Six hours of daily walking on cobblestones (uneven and broken cobblestones) most of the time, and the goodly amount of uphill and downhill we had to endure, made this tour of Italy difficult for me.

DAY 1 *Got to our rooms about 1:00 p.m. and, outside of dinner, no other events scheduled. We quickly learned the inadequacies of the Roman toilets, taking showers without curtains (the whole bathroom became a swimming pool), use of linen towels which did nothing for drying off, cot-sized beds, and going to the bar with our fellow travelers to get, not only a drink, but coffee.*

We were thirteen people: three married couples, five single ladies or widows, one widower and our tour leader, Father P., priest of St. Jude's Church in Twin Oaks, Florida, south of Ocala. Father P. was a most unusual person. He had been a N.J. cop and detective for many years, and was engaged to be married when he decided to fulfill a long-time desire to become a priest. In his mid-30s he joined the Augustinian Fathers because he could not find a seminary to accept him. Now, of course, there are several institutions especially set up to handle older vocations. After about twenty years in the monastery, he sought the opportunity to become a parish priest. Father P. was full of humor, getting along fairly well with the Italian language, could tell some great Irish jokes in dialect, loved to sing semi-classical songs, and was certainly "another Christ" when celebrating Mass.

Weather the whole time was pleasant sunshine—in the 70s—with rain only two nights after we retired.

Our Mass on September 26th was something to remember. There are forty-seven chapels under St. Peter's Basilica, around St. Peter's tomb. Each priest, leading a group of pilgrims, was assigned at one-half hour intervals. Each chapel was at the tomb of a saint, open on one side, and you could hear people all around us singing hymns in native languages. Many bishops were among them. It was impressive—

poignantly proving the universality of the Church. I was thrilled to be lector that day. All Masses had to be completed by 10:00 a.m. so that the Basilica could be opened to tourists.

The Sistine Chapel was like a subway rush hour. While much of the paintings were restored ten years ago, they are being redone with a new technique and chemical that makes the colors so brilliant and vibrant.

The Trevi Fountain, "Three Coins in the Fountain" was incredibly lovely. I had to skip the Catacombs and Coliseum and stay on the bus as the arthritis in my feet made walking almost impossible at the end of the day.

We attended a general audience of the Pope in St. Peter's Square on Wednesday morning. There were thousands and thousands of people there. Most of us had chairs. The Pope rode around in a jeep, circling so close to us the second time that one of our group shook his hand. He has the most beatific face—he already seems "not of this world." After an hour and a half speaking in about ten different languages (many times interrupted by groups singing hymns in native languages), he welcomed ten couples in wedding attire to come up to the podium, where he blessed them. Oh, after the Holy Father first arrived by helicopter, as he entered the square, an American Air Force band played "Stars and Stripes Forever"— very touching for us Americans.

DAYS 4 & 5 Assisi. My favorite place. Lovely flatlands in the lower town, steep hills *(reached by escalator—going up only) to the upper town where the churches of St. Francis and St. Clare were located. I did not realize St. Francis died at the age of forty-two and was canonized two years later. Here we stayed at a lovely hotel run by the Franciscan Fathers. There must have been over three hundred guests there. Lovely grounds, flowers. Rome is so devoid of green. Father P. said Mass both days—Saturday at a small stone chapel with lots of iron-work; Sunday at a chapel down in the original foundation, very beautifully designed, in St. Francis' Basilica.*

Two days in Florence—one day would have been enough for me. Traffic and crowds incredible, the walking a nightmare. Mass was held in the Church of St. Ambrose. A wonderful Italian priest-pastor of eight thousand people living in these five-story stone buildings, got us through the Mass. He spoke only Italian and had only Italian missals, so we ended up with a part-Latin Mass; our non-Catholic guide translated the epistles and gospels. All the steeple bells were rung. Then our host led us to his favorite restaurant in town, but could not stay since he had to say Mass for 500 university students.

Meals: Breakfast and dinner were provided daily. Plenty to eat, but not gourmet. Sometimes we could not tell whether the meat was lamb, veal, goat, or chicken. It was ample, with a course of two pastas first. We ate lunch in small groups, usually at pasta parlors. I ate loads of Italian ice cream—afraid of taking too many fluids until after the day's walking was over. Toilettes, when we could find them, were devoid of the usual things we take for granted like T. P., seats, towels, soap; many were co-ed and, outside of Rome, we had to pay to use them!

I could go on forever. Haven't even described the beauty of the marble churches, Roman artifacts and ruins. You have to go yourself! There was so much to absorb that I often felt there were no emotions left in me. I hope it has brought me closer to God. I know I have a greater love for our American way of life!

Love to all,

Feast of St. Francis of Assisi
October 4, 1996

ITALY
September 23–October 2, 1996

Rome

I only knew two things about foreign tour-group travel: you put your shoes outside your door every night so they could be shined by morning—never happened!

Secondly, you also put your suitcase outside your door by 6:00 a.m. That made sense. Your bus driver could have everything loaded and ready for the announced 8:00 a.m. or 9:00 a.m. departure. It was a better incentive than an alarm clock for getting up on time. If you didn't get your nightgown, change of clothes and toothpaste into your luggage, what were you going to do with them all day? Many tour schedules featured spending each night in a different town or city. When we stayed two nights in one place, it was heaven—and a temptation to skip breakfast.

What got me into this in the first place? Other than a faint desire to see Ireland some day, I never considered the possibility of foreign travel. But I had a persistent bug—named Marie—in my ear. We both worked on county school buses as aides to handicapped and disabled children. The buses would line up outside a particular school at a given hour each day. As we waited for our students to leave the building, there was time for visiting. Marie's bus parked behind mine. Early in 1995 she started to plan a trip to Italy and was a convincing sales person. Since I was newly-widowed and there was a year's time to save up the money, I decided this would be a morale picker-upper for me.

Returning to the topic of breakfast, this is a big item on these tours and, even if you are like me and do not eat a morning meal as such, you did so anyway. You did not know how many miles you were going to tramp before the next meal. Breakfast in Italy quickly converted me. Those big crusty rolls, with country fresh butter and luscious jams, were food for the gods. I skipped the eggs, cereals and meats to make room for a second roll.

When traveling as "a single," you learn to adapt to your assigned roommate's order of things, or lack thereof. On this trip my roommate was a lady in her eighties who traveled with suitcases bigger than she was. She could not lift them. Team work was required. Helen decided, since she was slow-moving, she would be the first one to get up, take her shower, and be out of my way when I got up. She set her alarm clock for 4:00 a.m. There was much rustling of paper as all her belongings were carefully folded into white tissue paper to prevent wrinkles. It was presumed that I could sleep another hour! Again, never happened! Before leaving, it took the two of us to sit on her suitcase to overcome the stubbornness of the zipper. Our morning exercise was often at 6:00 a.m. I admired her spunk, her good-naturedness. And she could hustle—to the bar for a martini—after we got back to the hotel at the end of a grueling day!

A few words about our 1) hotel accommodations and 2) social agenda. The answer to the second is none. The first was a very modest, old hotel on a side street in a "mom-pop store" environment. Our basic wants were taken care of, but there were not the amenities travelers expect. Inside the front door were three parlors, one opening into another where guests arrived and checked in, or if already registered, relaxed.

We were on the top floor under the peaked roof; the narrow hallway had rooms on one side only. Each room had a dormer window for light. It was a major undertaking to get one of the two elevators to winch you up the five stories. These elevators could hold two thin people and a suitcase (cut longitudinally).

The dining room was fairly large and unadorned. We gathered in a small coffee-cocktail lounge before and after our seven o'clock dinner. This was the recreational hub. Coffee, as well as drinks, was served there following the meal. Some of us hung around till closing at 10:00 p.m. The area was managed by a young couple. The woman was a Syracuse University student who had traveled to Italy for an abroad program her junior year, stayed, and married her young Italian lover. Very romantic— but shame on Syracuse—she could not make a martini. There were lots of volunteers to give conflicting directions on how "dry" was dry.

We all stayed together, never ate in a local restaurant, except for catching a lunchtime snack at a corner stand, and did not go out to see the night life. Most of us were so exhausted we did not mind. The billing was right: this was a pilgrimage to holy places, though I would not put Florence on my short list. I say these things now so you do not get bored. There are more fun trips coming up. Stay tuned!

I was not in shape for the physical demands of this tour. The bus would leave us off about 9:00 a.m. on one end of the city; we would walk all day through narrow streets and alleys until we met up with the bus on the other side of town about 5:00 p.m. Every couple of hours or so we would duck into a shop or store so we could use the rest rooms. I caught on to this ploy when we stopped at a beautiful, high-priced leather goods store. The tour guide whispered to us where the rest rooms were and, while we took turns, the others pretended to be engrossed in gorgeous purses worth about the price of our whole trip!

Nothing will ever match the excitement of landing in a foreign country for the first time! Seeing all the signs in a foreign language is an obvious and expected difference. Even mechanical apparatuses, like gates, baggage carousels and counters; color schemes, size, noise; everyone speaking in a foreign tongue—all become overwhelming. This is capped by converting one's money to lire—if you haven't done so back home—then being rushed through customs.

The next layer on the cake is wondering how we will meet up with our tour leader. Believe me, not to worry. They will find you! As you go though the final set of gates into the foreign world awaiting you, several dozen tour bus drivers and guides are holding up signs for your particular flight number, or sponsor, or point of departure from the U.S. Wasn't that easy?

To put the icing on this cake, we met our tour guide in this fashion. She herded us out of the airport buildings and we followed, dragging our luggage across four lanes of impossible traffic to a waiting bus. We were introduced to our driver. He was delighted to respond in English. We were then told our tip would be $2.00 American. What a shock to those of us who changed every last penny into lire! We soon found out that service people valued the American dollar. Our driver was saving his American money to help send one of his children to college in the States.

Before going further, I must remember to use the word "coach" or "motor coach" instead of "bus." It seemed to have a status symbol all its own.

Traffic in Rome lives up to its publicity. It's fast—almost reckless. Italian drivers are masters at spinning around traffic circles and spitting out at just the right fraction of a second into a side street. The cars are very small. They need to be, not only to get around, but to park. And they did park in almost impossible places. Once we started our walking sprints through cobblestone lanes, we learned to hug the buildings. It was not unusual to see tiny autos streaking like lightning down the lane behind us, keeping one set of front-back wheels on the cobbled sidewalk so a car coming the opposite way could pass. It must be mentioned that all of these driving machinations are accompanied by lots of horn blowing, and I mean LOTS.

We spent four days in Rome. In my letter I seemed to dismiss our visit to Vatican City almost as an aside. It wasn't. It was the highlight of our stay, as I am sure it is for most people. The first day we more or less hung out and slept. There was certainly no sleep possible on Alitalia Airlines. Everyone partied and drank, even sang, all night. Wine and cocktails (free) flowed like water. Some of the toilets backed up as we reached halfway across the ocean, and the stink was horrible. I was glad we were not sitting near them.

Speaking of the ocean, it is awesome (scary, too) to think one is flying across such a vast expanse of water, above 35,000 feet, with zero temperatures outside. Just a tiny speck in the sky. Who would ever find us? You knew you were in God's hands, or had better be. I couldn't take my eyes off the large electronic display at the front of the cabin that showed our route, where we were at any given moment, and the vital statistics connected with the flight.

I just have to insert here that the British like to call this "the big pond." I learned to fall in love with British understatements. It is part of their humor—despite "stiff upper lip and all that."

We visited various well-known churches such as the Church of St. Peter-in-Chains where we viewed Michelangelo's most celebrated sculpture of Moses. We also saw the Basilicas of St. John Lateran and St. Mary Major. I fell in love with St. John Lateran because of the most beautiful sky-blue ceiling I have ever seen. This church seemed brighter and more people friendly. Father P. offered Mass here twice. St.Paul Outside-the-Walls really is. Rome was once a walled city as were many cities in medieval times. Huge gates controlled the entering and leaving, and were shut at night, or in times of danger. We learned to look for the telltale signs of gates in other European cities.

Some of these churches may have no meaning for younger Catholics today but, when I was growing up, these churches were called "stations." The missal (prayer book for Mass) would always list at which station, such as St. John Lateran, the Mass would be held in medieval times. It meant that the Pope himself would offer a Solemn High Mass there. The people would assemble at a designated place and walk in procession to the church station, while singing psalms and chanting litanies.

A surprise for us Americans is to see ancient ruins on city streets surrounded by modern businesses and fast food places. Take the Pantheon, for example. This is probably the world's most famous building, with a hole in the roof- purposely built that way. It was meant as a link between the temple and the heavens. The Pantheon was built by Emperor Hadrian early in the first century as a temple to the twelve most important deities. The stone walls rise high above the surrounding modern-day residences.

St. Peter's Basilica, Rome

You must remember that these huge monuments and cathedrals were practically built by hand, with crude hand tools, and winches for lifting. To think they are still standing after almost two thousand years is beyond belief. They are super strong and super dirty (what wouldn't be after all that time)! There is nothing flashy or gaudy. The arches, curves, stained glass windows are tributes to the strength of man, and the beauty of his skill and, I would add, the beauty of his soul. They took decades, if not centuries, to build. Men spent their whole lives creating these masterpieces, as did their sons, and their sons who followed.

We finally got to Vatican City on our third day in Rome. With one hundred-nine acres, it is the world's smallest state, stuck right in the middle of Rome. It was established in 1929 and has its own postal service, currency, newspaper, and army, known as the Swiss Guards. The Guards were established in 1505 and still wear uniforms of red, yellow and blue, dating back to 1548, and said to be designed by Michelangelo. They patrol St. Peter's Square, guard the Pope at all times (when at home), and are stationed at the Vatican City gates. They are probably the most photographed men in uniform in the world! The young men are all from Switzerland, single, Catholic, between the ages of seventeen and twenty-five. They receive their room and board, plus about $1,000 a month, during their term of service.

I've got to clue you in on this before we take another step further. How do tour guides shepherd their flock in such huge crowds? They carry colorful umbrellas, folded, held aloft above their heads, while their group stretches out in a long line behind them. Some guides may even wear a distinctive piece of clothing, e.g. a green bowler hat, or an alpine outfit. They have huge voices, an occupational necessity. It is fun to see and hear them in closed places, like the airport, as one guide passing before you seems to echo what another group heard going the other way.

We had admission tickets for the Holy Father's Weekly Audience held outdoors in St. Peter's Square during good weather. Having a priest with us, who spoke Italian, gave us easy access. Father P. was invited to join an international group of priests sitting on the platform beside the Pope. A group of newlyweds also sat there. All were personally presented to the Holy Father at the end of the audience. This was great; Father P. filled us in on all we either missed, or did not understand.

Our group was seated just inside one of the waist-high fences about half-way back in the square. The Pope, standing in a jeep, came so close to us that one of our friends was able to shake hands with him. What a beautiful smile and rosy cheeks! It seemed truly heavenly. He was, of course, in fairly good health at that time. The audience lasted about one and a half hours.

Pope John Paul II greeted each national group in its own language. Many groups, dressed in native costumes, responded by singing a hymn in their native tongue; other groups cheered. When the United States was announced, an Air Force Band based in Germany, struck up "Stars & Stripes Forever." It made my blood run hot and cold with pride. I think every American there must have felt the same, even if he or she were not Catholic. This was a man of peace, and of God, being acknowledged in a very American way.

(This item conflicts with what I said in my opening letter. Our USAF band may have played at the arrival of the Pope, but I definitely remember wondering what would happen when the USA was greeted. Knowing how Americans act at baseball games, it was edifying that we put our best foot forward with Sousa's famous march.)

Later that day we visited two other outstanding places of interest: the Sistine Chapel and Vatican Museum and, secondly, the Trevi Fountain. But first, I must mention St. Peter's Basilica which was constructed between 1506 and 1626. The dome is famous—it can be seen all over Rome—all over the world, through the miracle of today's media. It is 138' in diameter and rises 452' above street level. Like most huge cathedrals in Europe, it is chairless! People stand through long hours of solemn religious ceremonies and account for the thousands of worshipers at one time.

I have seen so many pictures of St. Peter's that there were no surprises. The altar, with its four big columns at each corner, supporting a huge canopy, is quite well-known. There were many little chapels and altars in little niches around the outside walls. What was exciting though was to be able to descend to St. Peter's tomb below the main altar. My letter describes the lower level quite accurately.

The Sistine Chapel is famous for several reasons. We know it is the place where the College of Cardinals meet when it is time to elect a new pope, following the death of the old pope. You know what I mean. This chapel is quite small and is the site of the nine ceiling panels Michelangelo painted on his back, beginning in 1506. Twenty-two years later he painted the famous "Last Judgment." Over four centuries later, the frescoes were cleaned so as to restore their natural beauty and brilliance. While this undertaking was completed in 1994, work was still going on because a new, more modern technique had been found to be better. It was; the colors were awesome.

Exiting from the Sistine Chapel, one proceeds through long hallways in which huge tapestries are hung. Priceless art work by Botticelli, Roselli and Bernini adorn the walls, set off by Greek and Roman statuary from ancient times. One needs many visits to study and absorb it all. We are fortunate that so many of our library books depict these works, though it can't compare with being there in person.

When one talks about the wealth of the Church, it certainly included these priceless objects of art. The passage of time, the skill of the artists, the beautiful exposition and care, making them available for all to see, only increase their value.

I had to keep reminding myself that all I was witnessing existed because a little baby was born, cold, but much loved, in a stable surrounded by adoring parents and farm animals.

We concluded our sight-seeing by going to the Trevi Fountain. Surely you have heard the song, "Three Coins in the Fountain." The fountain and beautiful statuary surrounding it are so delicately and dazzlingly white! People gather here in huge crowds, day and night, mostly to "people watch" as we say in America. The legend says:

Throw one coin over your left shoulder into the fountain and you will return to Rome:

Two coins, you will fall in love;

Three coins, you will marry in Rome.

I threw three coins. I'll invite you to my wedding in Rome! Now, on to Assisi!

Assisi

On our fifth morning we left Rome and headed north in our motor coach to Assisi. The road was a super highway, with limited access, rolling past miles of grape arbors on the hillsides. Here and there were tiny little villages—probably the homes of the workers. Occasionally a huge, tall, stone house would be found. We presumed the owner, or a member of the aristocracy, might dwell there.

Our road was on a valley floor—fields set back from it for a couple of miles before the gentle slopes began. A railroad track, paralleling the highway, was often seen. The trip from Rome to Assisi took about four to five hours. We made one stop for lunch at a roadside fuel depot along the way. The countryside was known as Umbria.

As we neared our destination we could see, a few miles ahead, a high promontory with a road twining around the mountainside. This turned out to be the upper town of Assisi where St. Francis was born in 1182, and grew up in an affluent household.

The Portiuncula, Assisi, Italy

I am sure you have heard about St. Francis of Assisi—the son of a wealthy silk merchant who refused to follow in his father's footsteps in the mercantile world. Francis was quite a playboy in his youth. One day, however, a crucifix spoke to Francis, saying, "Francis, do you not see how my house is falling into ruin? Go and repair it for Me!" Francis thought he was to repair the crumbling walls of one of the churches, so he stole a horse and bolts of precious fabric from his father's store and sold them, offering the money to the priest who refused to accept it.

Francis' father denounced him in front of the bishop in the town square, whereupon Francis renounced his father by saying, "I am the son of God, not of man." The son then stripped off his clothes, handed them to the father and walked off into the forests and woods to live a simple, humble life, praising and serving God.

There are many stories about the gentleness of Francis, of how he talked to the birds and animals as they flocked around him. While walking through one of the many stone buildings, we came upon a sharp bend. There in front of us, in an outdoor setting, was a life-sized statue of Francis with several birds on his arms and shoulders. It was so striking!

Disciples, by the thousands, joined Francis in his life of abject poverty and humility. This was the start of his religious family, often referred to as Friars Minor. Within ten years there were five thousand brothers (Francis never became a priest) and they spread out over Europe and northern Africa, preaching a life of penance.

The Benedictines gave Francis a little church, called Portiuncula, which became the center and heart of his foundation. By age forty-two, Francis was weakened by malaria, malnutrition, tuberculosis, and an eye affliction. His body bore the stigmata—the wounds suffered to Christ's hands and feet on the Cross. Francis begged to die inside his beloved chapel of Portiuncula and so the monks carried him down to the valley and placed him before the altar.

This beautifully embellished little chapel now sits in the interior of the Basilica dedicated to St. Francis. His tomb is also there. Not far away is the Basilica of St. Clare. Clare was also a native of Assisi who wanted women to have the opportunity to lead a life of austerity, similar to the Friars Minor. Francis founded such a branch and placed Clare in charge.

As you walk around the upper town and see the same buildings that existed so many centuries ago, you can almost picture the merchants of that earlier day. Little souvenir stands, religious goods stores, small eateries now inhabit these structures. The streets are cobblestone, and hilly. As you climb up the long hillside towards the summit, the valley below is spread before you. One can look for miles over the fields below. On Saturday afternoon, we sat outside a small café in the town square and watched dozens of brides and grooms enter the city hall opposite, to be married civilly.

The Basilica of St. Francis, at the top of the long hill, seems to be a series of chapels and churches. They were beautifully adorned with priceless frescoes and paintings. I said "were" because the following year a series of earthquakes destroyed many of them.

We had lunch in a lovely restaurant, adorned with colorful flowers and seemingly perched at the edge of a cliff. It was one of the nicest and most relaxed moments of our trip. At the end of the day we returned to the lower town to a peaceful inn, hosted by the Franciscan Friars. This, too, was featured in a serene setting of lovely gardens and walks.

I felt that Assisi was the highlight of this tour. Its simplicity was appealing. Its history was more manageable for me than

that of Rome. I could more easily picture the life of the merchants in their stone dwellings than I could the gladiators in the Coliseum. The grandeur of the Sistine Chapel was just that—grand, beyond one's imagination
The fields, the hills of Assisi, praise God, too.

Florence

Assisi to Florence was yet another leap from nature, to the talent of man. Our last two days were spent in the city often titled, "The Jewel of the Renaissance." We approached Firenze, as it is known in Italy, from a long hill. There below us a river, featuring a plethora of bridges, stretched like a ribbon before our eyes. Dominating the skyline from any vantage point in and around Florence was the Basilica of S. Maria del Fiore. The duomo, with its cupola by Brunelleschi, was completed in 1240. Its campanile was designed by Giotto and the baptistry, with its incomparable bronze doors, by Ghiberti. One is not in Florence very long before realizing that you do not mention works of art here without attaching the name of the artist.

This is a city of not only outstanding and monumental Christian architecture and works of art, but also pays attention to Roman leaders, as well as gods of antiquity. Across from the palace, for example, is Cellini's statue of Perseus, Giambologna's "Rape of the Sabines" and Hercules. The world beats a path to Michelangelo's statue of David, dating from 1501. We were unable to gain admittance to the hall housing the original statue of David, because of the immense crowds and our tight schedule. However, an exact replica stands outside and we were able to capture its majesty on our cameras.

Everywhere one turns there are art exhibits, shops, and of course, elaborate churches and chapels. Religious triptychs might be exhibited next to buxom ladies in renaissance dress. Speaking of renaissance, we came upon the remnants of a medieval festival held on some side streets. Men were dressed in colorful silk costumes, featuring balloon pants, high ruffled collars, huge velvet berets with plumes. Their female companions were dressed in long gowns with tight waists, long sleeves, necklines of the period. There was much dancing, laughing, loud music, street musicians, etc. It certainly gave us the flavor of what Florence was like in the days of these famous artists.

We abruptly changed gears the second afternoon when we were told we had a few free hours to visit the flea market. Did they have flea markets in the 1500s, too?

We were nearing the end of our stay in Italy. It was a long drive back to Rome, since we had been heading north all week. We stayed overnight at a huge convent practically sitting on the edge of the airport. It had been a mother house for an order of nuns who fell on hard times (shortage of vocations, and donations, just like here). Rather than sell their beautiful estate and many buildings, they hosted pilgrims from around the world who had come to see the Eternal City.

This last night was memorable for me—my roommate awakened me in the middle of the night to say she was having a heart attack! Believe me, I would have propped her up in a plane seat and told everyone she was catching forty winks, if I had to. As it turned out, one of the nurses in our group assured Helen she was merely anxious about the flight ahead of us.

I am happy I made this trip. Now when I see a picture of St. Peter's Square, I remember exactly where I sat. I feel the spiritual warmth of a very special occasion in my life. But it is not one of the places that would draw me back for a return visit. Perhaps it was too profound! The gaiety, the light-heartedness, the group chemistry of future trips added a different dimension, as you will read.

IRELAND
June 27–July 9, 1998

Dear Family & Friends,

I hope to make this short enough that you will read it all...otherwise wait for the book! Or the movie! Or the TV Special!

Some facts, real & more real. Ireland is three hours wide, seven hours long, as the crow flies and as the Irish tell it. It would fit inside Maine and R. I. There are 254,000 miles of stone fences, 3,000 miles of coastline if you go around all the nooks, crannies, and inlets. 3,000,000 Irish are Catholics in the southern three-fourths of the nation; 1,500,000 Protestants in four counties in the northern section raising the devil.

Our tour statistics: George swears there are ten pubs for every three people; Mary Louise was sure she had been in 10,000 gift shops and only scratched the surface. Any church we saw was almost certain to be Protestant—snatched away from the Catholics centuries ago. Except

Galway Cathedral! What a beautiful church built, completely in marble (except for the seats, of course). We heard so much about Catholicism and saw no evidence of it—I felt I was in a pagan country. Last night, after Mass at PAFB, an acquaintance said they saw more Catholic churches in Israel than in Ireland.

There were forty-four people on the tour: two doctors (one an orthopedist, "in case we fall"), a couple of nurses, many teachers, and scads of people from California, Washington, and the mid-west. (Did they close down the west coast?) The youngest was Sean at eighteen; the trip was his graduation present. The oldest we called "Mama," she was ninety-four, traveling with her son and daughter. She kept up with the best and rest of us, though did take one day off to rest up. Eileen, my niece and traveling companion, was the next youngest at thirty-three—the darling of the tour. Several people told me how much they loved her vivaciousness and beauty. So many times she reminded me of my sister, Cathie, especially when she was in earnest about a topic of discussion.

Eileen "mother-henned" me so much in the beginning I felt I must have seemed like a hundred years old to her. She said later my pace-maker frightened her. She didn't know how much I could do. I also rather think, since she cared for my ill sister for so long, she compared me to her. Eileen was a great roommate, very generous in treating me to lunch, drinks, a steak dinner and so easy to live with.

We arrived Sunday noon (6/28) at Jury's Hotel in Dublin. Oh, all the hotels were very luxurious, all had indoor swimming pools, saunas, hot tubs, and fitness centers rivaling ours. The rooms were large, complete with very hot water, irons, hair dryers, electric pant pressers and electric hot water pots with the fixings for tea or coffee.

The first night we had dinner and cabaret at our hotel. Tony Kenney's show plays in Melbourne, Fl. every Christmas, with the same cast we saw in Dublin—cloggers, comedians, band, etc. It seemed strange to see them on their home soil.

The second night we passed up dinner and play at the Abbey Theater so we could visit a friend of your Uncle Denis. They were so poor by our standards (that's a whole story in itself) that it set my mood for the next few days. On our first day out of Dublin we went to Cobh, the embarkation point for all the Irish, emigrating to the U. S., from the time of the famine in the 1840s. A life-size exhibit put us in the hold of a ship with people dressed in rags, crowded onto sleeping racks, or sitting on the floor, sick, cold, shivering, while outside were the sounds of a raging gale at sea. We experienced how it felt to be on deck in such a storm. At the end there was a memorial to the approximately one hundred seventy-five Irish who boarded the Titanic at

Cobh—the first stop before England. A list of known Irish survivors included "Mrs. Mary Glynn." Mary Glynn is a name constantly seen in my Dad's family. (Alan, I hope you can track this down.)

We followed this up with a ride around the "Valley of the Famine," where thousands and thousands died of starvation right in the fields and on the roadways. Remnants of stone cottages were all around, tons of stone on the ground. The huts were rather far apart and, of course, there was nothing to do but work, harvesting potatoes. But in 1845-46-47 the crop failed and caused the wide-spread death. It was a real downer to realize our ancestors lived like this—work during daylight then go to bed. No wonder they drank so much, and made babies!

As to food on our trip: we all found it to be very bland and disappointing. By the second week, however, I began to accept it as a fact of life. Every meal—underline every—we were served carrots and boiled potatoes. A second veggie was also served—one day beans, and all the other days, broccoli. There was an appetizer, soup, entree, and dessert, which was not sweet. Eileen ate cheesecake every meal in order to find the right one. The first one was made out of gelatin; she worked up to one made with sour cream, and so on. I think oatmeal must have been the crust. I came home as a swimming pig. Salmon and pork appeared on every menu. The fields are covered with thousands of sheep—we ate lamb and beef only once.

Breakfast is a production: juice, porridge, bacon/sausage with eggs, then the toast (don't try to get it ahead of time), tea and coffee. All food was piping hot—now I know where my mother got that idea from! Salt was often served in salt cellars just like I grew up with (wish Cathie were around to tell these things to) - you take a pinch of salt between your fingers from a small bowl and sprinkle on food.

Will take a break here and reorganize my thoughts. Hope this fits on one page.

Love,

July 12, 1998

Part II

An historic one-liner: Corned beef and cabbage is strictly an American invention. Irish never heard of it.

You can keep Guinness beer. THE drink of Ireland. Dark brown, very bitter, you can cut it with a knife and fork.

I'm watching the Tour de France tonight. Sorry, only six hundred pubs for 1,000,000 Dubliners, according to ESPN. On our first three or four days we rode the Tour de France route; there were signs everywhere saying the roads would close at 8:00 a.m. on July 12th. The roads were great—Ireland got appropriations to bring them up to standard. It is a great boost for the economy.

Speaking of economy: one Irish dollar is equal to anywhere from $1.41 to $1.61 US dollars. So it is expensive to tour there. There is no tipping, except the bellmen. We gave them one punt (Irish dollar) to bring the bags to the room. We were asked to tip the Irish tour director, Noreen (a middle-aged lady with three grown sons and a daughter, very knowledgeable, full of Irish stories and legends); and our driver, Michael $3 American each, per day. (Italy was the same.) Extra tours, which we skipped, were over $200. All in all, the tour came to about $3,000. If I had known that in the beginning, I would probably have said no. Eileen's generosity helped a great deal. By necessity, I had to keep postcards and souvenirs to a minimum. But it was well worth it.

One of the missing pieces in a trip of this sort is that we meet very few Irish locals, outside of the hotel staff. Eileen and I had lunch at a local restaurant and invited a couple to sit with us, since it was so crowded. We gave up on understanding the middle-aged husband. The wife, after asking her to repeat her statements several times, we could communicate with. One smiling (very unusual) waitress in Sligo won our hearts. The last day I asked the waitress for two slices of bread to take home to a fellow Eucharistic minister at PAFB. She brought me a whole loaf.

The Irish are super polite and work hard. Store merchants open at 8:00 a.m., close from 1:00 - 2:00 p.m. for lunch, and work until 6:00 p.m. Two or three times I had hotel staff tell me not to worry about a bill, "what's a few pounds more or less," a very haphazard way of collecting money for their employers. The tourism industry works five months a year, May through September; even the biggest hotels close after the season is over. This makes for a poor economy since there are no other opportunities for so many.

My favorite places were Ring of Kerry, Killarney, Donegal. Eileen was so enamored of the country that she wants to return, buy a house, and settle down. Not me. Vermont is as green, and lovelier, in many places. Ireland's highest peak is 3,299 ft. and we have Mt. Mansfield!

I will close with mention of their famous shrine: Our Lady of Knock. In the 1870s fifteen people were walking past the church to see a lady down the road who was dying. An apparition—Mary, Joseph, and St. John the Evangelist—appeared on the church wall, lasting three or four hours. One of the men went for the priest, but the housekeeper wouldn't let him in; the priest was too tired from spending time at the dying lady's bedside. When the priest did hear about it, the apparition disappeared.

A beautiful life-sized replica has been built against the wall and enclosed by glass. Pope John Paul visited the site a few years ago and designated it "a universal shrine worthy of devotion." It was the only time we got to Mass in Ireland and we all were thrilled that we had the opportunity.

I'll let you read about all the well-known places we visited. I have tried to give you my reactions and feelings. It will live in my heart the rest of my days.

And now, all of you, save your money and come with us next year to Austria, Germany and maybe Switzerland. You all know how much I want to do that!

I'm off to Troy, N.Y. and Newport, VT. on Thursday. Back September 1.

Love to all - especially the little ones!

IRELAND
June 27–July 9, 1998

This was a great day for the Irish, March 17th, St. Patrick's Day. Every New Yorker was Irish on that day. There was a big parade on Fifth Avenue and there was no school—at least for Catholic schools. We did our best to get a good viewing spot right in front of St. Patrick's Cathedral, where the lane dividers were painted green. Cardinal Hayes stood on the cathedral steps, and all the bands played at their loudest and best, dipping their flags as they passed by. Numerous military units and college bands thrilled the parade viewers with Irish songs; hundreds of "New York's finest" police and firemen marched in close formation. The big thrill was the cadre of police horses that pranced so magnificently. There was happiness and gaiety everywhere.

The day before, our school held a St. Patrick's Day Party, a great departure from the normal school routine. We brought fancy cupcakes and other delicacies from home. Each classroom decorated a large table in the gym where we sat and ate. Irish records were played on the old crank-type victrola. There was an Irish sing-along. The nuns departed from their strict, dark, glum appearance by wearing a green ribbon on their sleeves This little bit of indulgence seemed to brighten their spirits, as much as it did ours. What fond school-girl memories!

My maternal grandparents were Irish, yet I never heard them mention Ireland. They were very American, though my grandmother did have a few odd Irish phrases she used. I don't know which generation before them emigrated. The only Irish reference I remember was a hush-hush mention of the Irish Sweepstakes. I gathered it was a huge yearly lottery which "the sons and daughters of Erin" spread throughout the world. I often wondered if it was legal here in the U.S. I remember my grandmother (a Crowley) speaking proudly of Jim Crowley, member of the Canadian Parliament, but I do not know their relationship. My grandmother died when I was a high school junior.

So now the big question: why did I want to visit Ireland and what did I expect it to be like? I was curious to learn what was left unsaid by my family. I knew the Irish famine in the 1840s was a huge disaster. I enjoyed childish stories about the leprechauns. The people were known for their wit, their drinking, their large families. Men married late, if at all. They hated the English who had taken their churches, their lands. They were devoted Catholics. My family could claim Archbishop Oliver Plunkitt, beheaded for the faith by the English, as one of our own. He was canonized by the Holy Father as St. Oliver only a few decades ago.

What to expect? I had no idea. I knew the country was very green and very rainy. I loved Irish music.

My niece, Eileen and I met in the Atlanta airport. We sat silently eating ice cream cones, staring into space, not knowing what to say to each other. We had only met twice before but, when Eileen heard I was going to Ireland, she phoned and said, "I am going with you."

Our flight was uneventful. It was easy to find our tour guide, Maureen, at the Dublin Airport. We chose to land at Dublin, instead of Shannon, where most tours start out, so that we could meet a friend of your Uncle Denis on the second night. As I mentioned in the family letter, we stayed at Jury's Hotel and enjoyed the cabaret show which Tony Kenney brings to Melbourne, Fl. every December. It was so great to see these performers here in their native land! We met a dozen or so of our travel mates seated around our table and right away knew this was going to be a memorable trip. A hobby of mine is to figure out what new acquaintances do for work. Immediately I nailed George to be a priest—he was so solicitous about making sure that latecomers, like Eileen and me, were served the salad and wine. He kept his eye out for all of us at the table, apprising the waiter what was needed. We were right about one thing—he loved to joke, assumed a degree of leadership in the group—but George had already been married four times, I believe. The laugh was on me.

Next morning we found our way to the motor coach at 9:00 a.m. and met the rest of our fellow passengers. We were forty-four in all. Eileen and I sat about halfway back in the bus. Maureen counted noses and found that one person was missing. "Oh, that's my wife," said the fellow across the aisle from Eileen. We waited and waited, finally a well-dressed figure entered the bus and sat down. The "wife" had a huge, blond, handlebar mustache about as wide as his head, and as bushy. Suddenly everyone was looking the other way, thinking of something to distract, or tell a joke. We were not familiar with this life-style. They were a very nice couple, but pretty much kept to themselves.

We took off on a happy note. Almost everyone was Irish and may have had parents or grandparents who were born there. One family had a brother still living in Ireland. We were touched at their family reunion. The mood was light-hearted;

there was much joke telling and camaraderie. Immediately upon leaving the hotel we found ourselves on Embassy Row. Even though we had arrived only a day ago, seeing the American flag flying outside our U.S. Embassy was a thrill.

Dublin is the capital of Ireland. Its government buildings were made of grey stone, not overly pretentious, situated on neat and well-landscaped grounds. We visited St. Patrick's Cathedral where Jonathan Swift was once Dean, and then on to Trinity College, home of the magnificent 8th century Book of Kells. We spent quite a bit of time on O'Connell Street, the shopping center of Dublin. Vehicular traffic was excluded and so one could enjoy a wide promenade while freely crisscrossing from one boutique to another. It was amazing how noisy and crowded it was.

That evening will stand out forever. We were invited to dinner at the home of a man named Michael and his family. When I asked your Uncle Denis recently how he knew the man, he emailed the following message:

"In August 1972 Robert McIntosh and I left for Ireland to work for Desmond Guinness of the Irish Georgian Society to assist in restoring old castles and country houses." (Denis and his friend Bob were architectural majors at R.P.I., Rensselear Polytechnic Institute, Troy, N.Y., at that time.) *"We lived and worked at Castletown House for two months before Desmond 'sub-contracted' us to Michael.*

"Michael was (and, apparently, remains to this day) an eccentric architect with a large collection of military uniforms that was to provide Henrietta Street the basis for non-profit status. At least half of our time with Michael was spent in walking tours about Dublin and drinking tea at the Russian Tea Room.

"Meanwhile, at Henrietta Street, at least six poor families were living in various rooms of the house and sharing a single

loo at the end of the 2nd floor hallway. Our task was to remove modern walls that divided each major room into a dwelling unit. A more delicate job was to chip thick layers of paint off ornate plaster ceilings (labeling each piece of plaster ornament that fell off and storing it in a cigar box). Our favorite caper was, in the dead of night, to remove from an abandoned country house two rooms of antique oak paneling for reuse at Henrietta Street (a procedure quietly approved by Desmond himself).

"I believe Michael is now a consultant to movie producers on historic detailing of movie sets."

Eileen and I received a call from Michael's wife, Aileen, to meet their oldest son at the Central Post Office. She was confident it would be easy to find each other. Guess we Americans stand out more than we think. We took a taxi to reach that destination. Instead of his son, Michael came up and introduced himself. He said that, since it was such a fine afternoon, we would walk to his home. We walked, and we walked, and we walked…almost an hour. It was easy to understand why Michael's shoes were coming apart at the seams. We later learned that they did not have a car; that the six children had never been further from home than whatever distance they could reach on foot.

We were getting curious as we proceeded from business and commercial neighborhoods to what could only be called tenement housing. Just as we reached a street that looked more run-down than the others, we approached a three-storey row house without a door knob, and almost without a door. One reached in a little hole and unlatched it from inside. Stepping beyond the threshold, we saw the plaster walls stripped through varying layers of paint of different colors. The ceilings must have been fifteen feet high. Michael took us step by step through each room on each floor, lecturing non-stop about the past history of the building.

By 8:00 p.m. I was exhausted and begged to sit down…and I was starving. I could not figure out why there were no chairs in the dining room. We still had not met Aileen or any of the children. Finally, I broke away and found the hostess in the smallest kitchen in the world. It held a card table with odds and ends of plates and cups, a three-burner hotplate and a fridge waist high like a dorm model. There was one bare bulb hanging from the ceiling, one cold water tap perched over a dishpan. That was it. Out of that kitchen came the most heavenly Irish stew in the world, and an apple pie, with freshly made whipped cream, that the angels must have made. What a feast!

There was much scuffling as the boys brought in chairs from the outside, probably from the neighbors, we thought. There were wine glasses, lovely china and silver, and candlelight. The only other light in the house was in the second floor bathroom, "the loo," as Denis said. (Eileen and I made the trip up to the bathroom before dark so we would not have to carry a candle to find the way.) We were invited into the cellar where Michael had assembled a computer from spare parts. I let Eileen cover that assignment by herself, as this undertaking was by candlelight also.

Lakes of Killarney, Ireland

The four boys and two little girls ranged from four years to about eighteen. The boys all attended the Catholic school nearby. They looked freshly scrubbed, had the rosy cheeks and bright blue eyes so typical of the Irish, and were wearing their school uniforms. The oldest boy was very interested in art and wanted to study in Rome, His teachers, the Benedictine Fathers, were going to give him room and board at their house in Rome as their donation towards a scholarship program for him. Aileen, herself, was an accomplished professional in commercial design and layout, I believe, but Michael would not hear of her working. She had little to say when he was around. We also had to coax some conversation from the youngsters who seemed awe-struck by meeting Americans, staying up late, and having "seconds" for dinner.

Michael seemed to be unemployed at the time, but we did hear about his several trips to Hollywood to work as a consultant. This was hard to figure out, but Denis' letter above explains it.

Wine flowed like the River Shannon. It was a fantastic evening. We got the impression that the whole month's food budget was spent on this one meal, and that the neighbors had a hand in supplying the tableware. The family's hospitality was overwhelming. Their pride and dignity, in the midst of what seemed like abject poverty, added to their poise.

We left at 10:00 p.m. in daylight, and let Michael escort us to the nearest intersection where we could catch a cab. He seemed flabbergasted that we would resort to such transportation.

I still receive a yearly Christmas card from Michael and his family of Dublin, Ireland!

Now our tour of Ireland began in earnest. One of our first stops was at an old castle in ruins in the Wicklow Mountains near Glendalough. There was a very tall stone tower standing alone in a field. It had rough openings for light and air, but no visible means of entry. There was a purpose to that. When enemies arrived to sack the area, the home folks would climb a ladder to get inside the tower and pull the ladder in after them. Then they would pour boiling oil on the enemy below!

A stop at Waterford is mandatory. It is the home of the world-famous Waterford Crystal Factory where glass is still hand-blown, and etchings are done by hand. It is an intriguing and time-consuming process. As we toured the plant, we were invited to stop and have our pictures taken while holding a huge Waterford pitcher. I was so afraid I would drop it. We were promised the picture upon departure. They did not say it was for a price, but who would refuse. We might never come this way again.

We spent two nights in Killarney. All these famous places, familiar to those who love Irish melodies, came alive. The Lakes off Killarney are actually one lake that seems to have two halves spilling into each other much like Lake Eden in Vermont, that your parents know so well. The water was heavenly blue and the green mountains coming down to the shore line actually imitated The Green Mountains of Vermont.

We visited Blarney Castle, but Eileen did a solo on that one. A narrow stairway inside a dark castle tower wound up to the Blarney Stone, where one kneels down and hangs over a cliff backwards, and kisses the stone. (Someone holds your feet while you do this!) Too much for these bones. You have heard of the Blarney Stone, I am sure. It is said that, when someone talks too much, it is because he kissed the Blarney Stone. Here we also found the Blarney Woollen Mills. Ireland is so renowned for its knitted goods. Aran sweaters from the Aran Islands are famous. "Fisherman knit" would reference these hand-made treasures.

Cobh followed and I would refer you to my opening letter about this famous wharf from which the Titanic picked up its first passengers.

We went through Cork and I do not remember a single thing about it except that Blarney Castle was nearby. I was reminded that my grandmother's family was from County Cork but had no idea about names and places, even if I had an opportunity to search the city.

While we are talking about world-renowned Irish crafts, let me skip ahead to Donegal, site of the Belleek China Company. Every article, from ashtrays to platters to dinner ware, is hand-made. It was so interesting to watch the item start out like soft clay and, through many hand processes, end up glazed and hand-decorated. Many Belleek items feature a three-dimensional braid design, almost their trademark. (Ask your parents to show you the small oblong dish I sent them.) These items could have been turned out so much faster on a mechanized assembly line, but that is American thinking. These craftsmen were very proud of their skills, and rightly so.

I must insert here mention of marble products and fine Irish lace. We stopped at a very small one-man marble factory. Actually, the store front was filled with souvenir-style marble artifacts. (I bought a small marble-handled butter knife made of Connemara marble.) The shop owner had tools and machines back stage to shape chunks of marble into these marketable items.

Have you heard the expression, *lace curtain Irish*? I have often wondered if this is an American saying, indicating a family is on its way up the social and financial ladder. I would not say this lace is as famous as Belgian lace, but it has its respected place in the craft world.

You must go to Tralee! It was our next stop after Killarney. The most fantastic exhibit is found in the basement of a small stone building, facing a tiny common. The building was about the size of a small-town post office, and the common was a mass of roses in bloom. So many colors! Such picture-perfect formation.

Inside the building we first climbed the stairs to a second floor museum of pictures and documents. Then down two flights to the basement. I cannot do justice to this exhibit. We mounted small cars on a little track (like a kiddie amusement ride) and wound back and forth through life-sized street scenes of olden times. The exhibit seemed to be a replica of perhaps, a castle's nether regions, where the cooking was done, where the servants did the laundry and other chores for the lord residing above. There were huge cauldrons of stew and vegetables with accompanying steam and aromas. There were big fires, in open fireplaces, where more cooking was taking place. The voices of servants, yelling back and forth, filled the air. The lighting was dim—candlelight, of course. Life-sized wooden cobblers, candle makers, and butchers in authentic costumes added more life and sound to this exhibit. This is a must-see!

As we drove out of Tralee we saw many buildings with thatched roofs—an historic reminder of the peasants cottages of one and two centuries ago. This theme was carried out in many other villages. We stayed a night in Limerick, famous for its Georgian architecture. The Bunraty Castle and Folk Park are big sightseeing places in this area. The Cliffs of Moher are also quite famous— huge cliffs dropping straight into the sea. People say it is always raining there, but no doubt because of the heavy mist and spray. It's a rather gloomy place.

Crossing into County Galway we stopped at Rathbaun Farm to see sheep being sheared, to have lunch at a converted barn, and admire the government-sponsored model little settlement surrounding it. I didn't think there was much excitement to this stop, but then I have seen sheep sheared before, and have been in many a working barn.

We stayed in Connemara on Galway Bay. Do you know the lyrics, "when the sun goes down on Galway Bay"? A native said this only happens in November. It was picturesque, in a stark sort of way. While the hotel was on the water's edge, one had to pick one's way over big black stones and marshy, squishy areas, to actually reach the bay. It is a wild land of rocky mountains. We already had driven for hours through the Burren, a strange, lunar-like area, petrified in carboniferous limestone. After dinner, we gathered in the hotel lobby to watch an Irish lass perform her native dances.

Eileen & Tinker outside Donegal, Ireland

Irish Jaunting Car - Eileen & Me

The best lunch of the whole trip was at Kylemore Abbey— a neo-Gothic mansion of seventy rooms, built by an Irish nobleman for his bride. It is now owned by an Irish Benedictine community of nuns who operate an exclusive girls' boarding school, with students from all over the world in attendance. There was an authentic Gothic chapel, facing directly on a beautiful lake, backed by mountains. Our superb meal was cafeteria style in a small dining room on the grounds. One could spend days here in this lovely, peaceful, heavenly setting.

I've already mentioned the Shrine of Our Lady of Knock and the Galway Cathedral in this area. There are so many other sights I have not yet mentioned. Let me list a few of them—one could write many pages about each one.

1. Muckross House, built in 1843 in Kerry by a Member of Parliament. It sits on 11,000 acres, hosted many notables,

including Queen Victoria. It was eventually bought by a member of the Guinness Brewing Family. They used it for hunting and fishing parties. In 1911 a wealthy American bought it for his daughter as a wedding gift. When she died in 1929, the family donated the estate to the Irish nation and it became Ireland's First National Park.

2. The Valley of the Famine in Kerry, where many thousands died of starvation during the potato famine of 1845–46–47. It is said that dead bodies would be found alongside the roads and in the fields. Here, in this agricultural area, one saw remnants of stone cottages where these people had lived. There were piles of huge stones and boulders. In order to make room for the sheep to graze, these boulders were piled into stone fences, which are still standing today. This famine caused many survivors to emigrate to the United States to seek a better living.

3. Sheep...everywhere. Motor coaches would stop to let them cross the roads as they meandered at will. The meat is a big export for the Irish people. As I mentioned earlier, we only ate lamb once during our whole stay.

4. Tinkers on the country roads. Some had little carts, or beat-up travel trailers, or wagons for housing on the side of the road. They are a gypsy-like people looking for handouts, perhaps offering music as an incentive. We took a picture of Eileen and a tinker, dressed in kilts, blowing his bagpipes on a high country road in the mountains near Donegal.

5. Irish jaunting cars. If you have seen the movie, *The Quiet Man*, you will remember the little carts drawn by donkeys. The passengers sit back-to-back, facing the side of the road. Hacking is a way of life for many men who have retired from more active farming occupations. Eileen and I certainly enjoyed the little old Irish gentleman who drove us around. We felt we belonged in that movie too!

6. Gift Shops...too numerous to count. Very beautiful shops, I might add. No two alike—no big gift chain—but small mom-and-pop operations. Their Irish wares are so lovingly displayed. I am not one to even enter a department store unless I am dragged, but this is another whole scene.

7. Pubs. One night in Connemara, I believe, our group went to a local pub to have a few drinks and hear a native performer sing native songs—not the Irish songs we Americans feature around St. Patrick's Day. Eileen fell so much in love with the atmosphere, situated near a fishing wharf, she was ready to buy a house in Ireland where we could spend our summers and she could one day use as her retirement home.

A very touching experience for all of us. As we came out of our hotel in Limerick to start a new day, the motor coach was adorned with red, white, and blue crepe paper, and balloons. It was the Fourth of July! Everywhere we went that day, sales clerks, waitresses, and other service people wished us "Happy Fourth of July!" They knew how much this day meant to us and to their family members who had emigrated to the USA.

We were blessed our whole trip with almost no rain. Just a few light showers late at night. It would be easy to find scads of people who would not believe this.

As we drove north towards Donegal, we passed by the borders of Northern Ireland. We were told that our motor coach might be stopped by the authorities and they would confiscate any cameras they found. In fact, it has been told that the camera's owner might be forced to leave the bus. No one knows what happens after that. I had hoped we would visit Belfast, because of its renown, and Armagh, where my ancestor, Oliver Plunkitt, was archbishop before being imprisoned and killed by the English.

Donegal was my favorite place because of its spectacular scenery. It reminded me so much of the Green Mountains, of the areas around the Worcester Range, and the road from

Waterbury to Burlington, Vermont. But I had to wonder what people did there. What did the young folks do for fun and amusement? Perhaps it was still home-grown entertainment like their ancestors engaged in: barn dances, fiddling contests and the like. It was so rural and isolated.

The tour ended with a straight shot south, from Donegal and Sligo, to Dublin in one day. As I pointed out earlier, Ireland was only seven hours long as the crow flies, and Dublin is not even at the southernmost part. We did stop en route in Boyne Valley to view neolithic tombs. They were said to predate the pyramids by more than 1,000 years. This was boring to me, but many people really enjoyed the antiquity.

That last evening thirteen of us gathered for a final dinner and drinks at our hotel, although the tour was officially over. We exchanged addresses, cracked a few more jokes, and promised to keep in touch. Little did Eileen and I know that this was the jolliest, most fun-loving, friendly group we would ever travel with. It became the standard by which we have judged all subsequent trips we have taken together.

Our itinerary was jam-packed with so many interesting and fun things to see and do that we never noticed the miles in between. Eileen and I still talk about returning some day.

I would like to end this with the first verse of a poem found on the cover of the Galway Cathedral Newsletter:

"Slow me down, Lord.
Ease the pounding of my heart by the quieting of my mind.
Steady me with the vision of the eternal reach of time.
Give me, amid the confusion of my days, the calmness of the everlasting hills.
Break the tensions of my nerves with the soothing of the streams."

"The calmness of the everlasting hills"—is that the key to my soul? Yes!

CENTRAL EUROPE
Munich, Prague, Vienna, Salzburg
June 11–21, 1999

Dear Family & Friends,

We were an un-cohesive group of twenty-seven, three from Australia, a couple from South Africa, a lady from British Columbia, the rest were Americans. Eileen and I could not help comparing this group with the people who went to Ireland. Then, there was plenty of camaraderie, joking, teasing, laughing, practical jokes, getting together spontaneously in the lounge—like a junior high class on an outing. This time everyone kept to himself and his partner and did not intermingle. You could hear a pin drop in the bus.

Our tour director was Dutch, a very tall, attractive woman in her 40s who has taken groups all over the world. Eileen found her very dictatorial—if anyone was three minutes late, we got a lecture on discipline. That paid off later. But I enjoyed Margareitt, and her

Germanic temperament was what I would expect.

We got up at 6:00 a.m. almost every morning. Margareitt wanted to be the first bus at the next event. When we went up to Eagle's Nest (Hitler's hide-out in the mountains), we were the first group up the mountain and enjoyed a beautiful view. By the time we returned to the ground, the mountain had fogged in and passengers from at least fifteen busses were milling around. Likewise, on our cruise up the Danube, at first we had the whole cruise boat to ourselves. At subsequent stops we quickly filled up.

Our hotels were top of the line, usually a Sheraton or Radisson, but did not have the amenities of Ireland, i.e. no in-room coffee pot, iron, ironing board or pants presser (except the latter in Munich). The tubs were so high I had to forego a shower in two hotels. (Afraid to break a hip after I had one good slip.) We saw a blanket only once. All the beds had a futon on top, which one spread over himself. It was very heavy and hot. The temp. everywhere was in the 70s—we needed a sweater morning and night.

Meals opened with soup...mostly mushroom. No salad ever. Then schnitzel, or a platter of different wursts (our first night), goulash, chicken filet once. Plenty of beer—sometimes it was included, otherwise we paid for it. And wine available at an extra price. Veggies were not plentiful. A few string beans, potatoes and, *of course, noodles. There was always dessert, a piece of cake, pudding etc. I had a " sacher torte" at a lunch stop one day—liked the Trapps variety better. Also tasted the dark bread–very like Hedwig's. But the Arabella Radisson in Munich had super "muesli" (oatmeal gravy— my term, because it is thicker than a sauce - over fruit). The Trapps must have cheated on the heavy cream on that one.*

The most bounteous, artistic, breakfast buffet was in Munich. Beautifully decorated canapes, every conceivable croissant, roll, bread and jams you could imagine. The smoked salmon was out of this world! Couldn't wait for our return to Munich to have more. Cold cuts were served at breakfast, but trying to get a sandwich at lunch was almost impossible. Two other younger girls (ages twenty-five and thirty-five) made up a foursome with Eileen and me. We often looked for a TGIF or a Pizza Hut for lunch. McDonald's is everywhere! Also saw Burger King.

Most tourists like to shop; we all thought our tour was poorly planned in that we spent two Sundays in Munich where all the stores were closed. We arrived in Salzburg at 3:30 p.m. on Saturday, and the shops there had closed at 2:00 p.m. I thought that was just an old-fashioned tale of Maria von Trapp. Eileen was looking for a cuckoo clock; only saw one shop in the airport that had a few. Like the non-existent Alps we were all looking for—we should have been in Switzerland. Once we got to Salzburg, we did see some of the snow covered mountains.

Money was a nightmare. Four countries— each with a different currency, and not accepting its neighbor's money—was something else. I could keep the Deutsche Marks and the Czech Republic money straight. By Hungary I was all mixed up; and by Austria I just put out my hand to a clerk and said, "help yourself." We had to exchange at each border in order to pay for lunch and toilets.

Border crossings were to be endured. Sometimes they kept us standing there for up to two hours. I think part of this was because non-Americans had to have visas. The authorities would pick these up, return them, and pick them up again. We avoided some of the horror stories, however, that Margareitt told us about other groups.

I'm going to sign off now so I don't lose this narrative again. Will continue later with Part II- the sights we saw, the places we went, etc.

Love to all—

via e-mail, June 25, 1999

e-mail June 26, 1999

We arrived in Munich Sunday noon. I was surprised at how modern, bright, clean everything was. So many beautiful glass, high-rise, buildings. Our hotel was in a lovely park, and surrounded by another half-dozen hotels. We got a brief tour through the city and had dinner at a local German restaurant; about six different kinds of wurst, with beer.

The next day was long, with a whole day on the bus, as we rode to Prague, Czech Republic. Went through Pilsen, an industrial city - huge oil storage tanks everywhere. The countryside was flat and green. We passed by lovely little farm towns that were off the Autobahn. All the houses had red roofs. The farmers go out to their fields from the town. Dinner at the hotel.

At night we had a "walking tour" through the old section of town, starting high at a hilltop monastery; taking a narrow-gauge tram down the mountain side, and then going to a hofbrau house for a drink and native music - only the accordionist played, "Oh, Susanna," "Beer Barrel Polka," (naturally), and a few other American sing-alongs as well. This was a paid excursion, in other words, extra charge, optional. There were about ten such trips at a charge of $50 - $75. All together they added up to $480. Eileen and I chose four and she insisted on paying for me. I think we were all surprised at the number and cost of these tours. In Ireland *we had only two, as I recall—one being a ride in a donkey cart!*

Prague is beautiful at night; so many bridges lit up like necklaces crossing the river. Since it does not get dark in that part of Europe until 10:00 p.m., these night-time trips ended close to midnight. Prague has many baroque churches. The population of the countries we visited is 70% Catholic, but only about 20% practice regularly. Unfortunately, we were unable to get to Mass on the Sundays. I had looked forward to this. They are known for beautiful choirs.

Two nights and days in Prague. I skipped one afternoon of sightseeing on our own in favor of resting my feet and knee. There were stairs everywhere—every public "john" was in the cellar, every group dinner in a restaurant was upstairs, and five very steep steps onto the bus. We got in and out of the bus at least four or five times daily.

Budapest was next. This was quite old-fashioned. Almost no one spoke English. They pretended not to know German. (I did very well with my German and was surprised at how much I remembered.) They seemed to regard tourists as intruders. Guess the idea of the tourist dollar had not occurred to them.

The city had lots of churches with the "onions" on top. Eileen and I spent one afternoon at the local "market" and got lost going back to the hotel. Violated all rules about not hiring a taxi driver, other than one at a hotel. We were constantly warned about pick-pockets and scams. One evening we had a dinner cruise on the Danube, which was lovely.

From Budapest, we went to Vienna, still very flat land, no mountains, which surprised us all. Eileen and I skipped a Mozart concert in Vienna—I have plenty of Mozart CDS—saving a big price tag. We toured all the government buildings, Parliament, Palace Gardens, etc. The buildings were quite impressive. Two full days there.

From Vienna to Salzburg we began to see some hills and mountains. In fact, it suddenly struck me how like Route 2, between Waterbury and Burlington, VT., the resemblance was. En route, we stopped to see Melk Benedictine Monastery, from the outside. It is quite huge and dominates the hillside. Father Jim Dodge always talked so fondly of this holy place (dates back to the 1300s) and he visited often - making retreats there. How I wish he were still alive to show us the real sights!

As we approached Salzburg, the tour director pointed out many spots where the "Sound of Music" was filmed (this church for the real one, this meadow was a substitute, etc.) I whispered to her my connection with the von Trapp Family. She asked my permission to tell our local tour guide when we reached Salzburg. Then she made an announcement to the whole bus. I became a minor celebrity.

Hate to do this, but I am sending this off now—just lost the last paragraph, and it is dinner time. To be continued.

Love to all. Hope you stick with me—

e-mail, June 28, 1999

Of course we reached Salzburg on Saturday at 3:30 p.m. and the stores closed at 2:00 p.m. I would really have liked to see some of the crafts here. We went through the "old section" of town, as usual, where the "new" buildings dated from the 14th century, and onward! These tours throw so many old dates and historical facts at you, you come away thinking America is a youngster without roots.

We went to the Getreidestrasse—a long cobbled street off which opened five big squares, or platz—filled with old churches, stores with living quarters over them, usually four stories high. They were very beautiful. We saw where Mozart lived as a boy in one of these apartments. We were told that, "He probably had the chore of emptying the chamber pots down on the street before the required 7:00 a.m. deadline."

An American Jr. H. S. orchestra was practicing in one of the churches. The squares were packed with tourists. Everywhere we went we met as many oriental tourists as we did Americans. Also true for the hotels. You wonder what these places look like in off-season.

We stayed at the Radisson out by the Salzburg Airport, and saw our first alp. Up again Sunday morning at 6:00 a.m. and off to Eagles Nest, a lodge built by Martin Boorman for Hitler. We took an elevator straight up 407 ft. to the one remaining building, the dining hall, now converted into a restaurant. Hitler did not like heights and only visited there about six times. The view was outstanding. You felt you had stepped out onto the wing of a plane, and looked down on the mountains and valleys.

On to Munich for our last night. We went to a beer hall—a huge place that could be Pennsylvania Station in New York City. Long wooden tables, an oom-pah-pah quintet, dressed in lederhosen (the only alpine costumes we saw). What music—loud, catchy, foot-stomping music! A final dinner at a German restaurant and back to the hotel to pack.

Rare meat is unheard of, except for good old TGIF coming up with a rare hamburger. Other thoughts: I forgot the Charmin! The toilet paper was the color and consistency of a paper towel in a gas station! No wonder no one smiles...I didn't either, some days.

Jackie—I wondered if you and Mike saw the real von Trapp Family house. They told us the surrounding neighbors complained about the traffic, and sightseers were "verboten." While I knew it all along, it certainly hit me hard that the Tyrolean costumes of the Trapp Family were merely a persona. They lived in an ordinary city, distant from the mountains, yodeling, dress, architecture, etc. of the Tyrol. It would be like the Lamours moving to another country, portraying a public image of cowboys.

I missed not getting to Mass. Was curious about the hymns that would be sung and if it would it remind me of the many religious festivities over which the von Trapp family presided.

Found I could order food in German, and ask directions. A great consolation to Eileen.

The highlights were the two cruises. Guess I have not said very much about Vienna. The big public buildings were spectacular and every street and square seemed to be laid out with great precision.

I am very happy I went. It will take time to sort out all the sights we saw, and all the things we did, and where. Hope to make up an album soon, and that will put things in perspective.

Do I want to go back? Certainly, to see the Tyrol and Switzerland, and parts of Germany a friend talks about, with roadside shrines, wood carvings, and small village goings-on.

There will be a quiz in ten minutes.

Love—

CENTRAL EUROPE
June 11–21, 1999

As our trip to Ireland wound down, Eileen and I talked about traveling together again. Eileen wished to see Nuremberg, where the famous trials against the Nazis were held after World War II. Her Dad was a U. S. Army officer stationed there at that time, and had described the scene to his family. It was also Eileen's birthplace.

I wanted to see Salzburg, Austria, the original home of the von Trapp Family, as well as Switzerland. The only trip we could find that included Nuremberg and Salzburg was the one on which we now embarked. Switzerland would have to wait.

As I read over the e-mails sent to my family, I am amazed that I did not even mention Nuremberg. It was the starting place for our travels, after we left Munich. We saw Hitler's headquarters—a mammoth stone building with huge columns. About a mile or two away was a gigantic stadium, many stories high, facing an immense cemented parade ground. If you ever see newsreel footage of Hitler reviewing his troops, it would no doubt show you this very site. Eileen climbed to the top of the reviewing stand; she appeared as a small dot.

We saw the remnants of a couple of wooden barracks, American or German, we didn't know. Eileen was disappointed that there was no big fanfare about the

"Nuremberg Trials" being held here. But that is understandable if you remember that we, the U. S., had been the enemy and the victor and the judge.

After this very short visit, we were off to Prague, via Pilsen, the industrial city I mentioned in the family letters. We spent several days in the Prague-Budapest area. Prague was truly a fairyland with turrets, towers, many bridges, tree-lined streets, domed churches and cathedrals. The "Blue Danube" was brown—a shocker. We thought, at least here, a river would be blue. But, like many other rivers famed in the musical world, pollution, civilization and industry have left an indelible mark.

Eileen underwent a frightening experience in Prague, She, and two other girls about her age, Candice and Helen, went shopping. They found a cute little gift ship off the beaten track and went in looking for wooden, etched eggs. Helen picked up a doll. She heard a thump and saw a fragile, painted eggshell, laying broken on the floor,. The two shopkeepers accused her of breaking the egg and insisted on her paying for it. When Helen refused, saying it was a set-up, they locked the door and turned away other shoppers. A threat was made about calling the police; there was a stand-off of over an hour. It then occurred to Eileen that maybe they might not be so safe in the hands of the police, so she agreed to pay with a credit card. The shopkeepers unlocked the door and, as Eileen went through the door last, one of the women punched Eileen in the side of the head. The girls fled, with the two shopkeepers following them, until they reached a main thoroughfare, got caught up in a crowd, and ducked into a restaurant.

I would call Budapest more quaint—not like parts of New England, or the Amish Country, are quaint—but perhaps "old world" would be better. There are two parts to Budapest, "Buda"on one side of the river, "Pest" on the other side of the

Danube. Buda dates from medieval times. A disastrous flood in 1838 all but wiped out Pest. It was quickly rebuilt, with many elegant hotels along the river front. In the years of 1944–45, Pest fell victim to the devastation of World War II.

Castle Hill, Buda, on which a fortress was built in 1255, followed by a royal palace and government buildings about two centuries later, is the heart of the Hungarian nation. The second World War brought tremendous devastation here, too. No more than one hundred-seventy buildings on Castle Hill survived. It was not until ten years after the war that the work of restoration got underway. The old style was retained when the houses, street and buildings, were restored. Today's visitor can enjoy the old beauty of the Castle District and see how it has managed to mirror the country's history in its stones. In 1988 the Buda Castle District was declared part of the World Heritage by UNESCO.

As I mentioned earlier, Budapest was not as people-friendly as other places we visited. Perhaps, "American friendly" could be substituted here—I don't know. As I also said, Eileen and I spent an afternoon at the local market, a huge building about the size of an airplane hangar, with stalls on two levels. Going back to the hotel, we got lost and flagged down a taxi on one of the back streets. When we gave the name of our hotel, the driver said he did not know it. I tried to describe it as well as I could in my rusty German, without success. The driver became so incensed that, when Eileen said we should get out and find another cab, the driver locked all doors. We began to get a bit panicky. I thought he might understand English, after all.

I asked the driver to go to the main street and drive around. We soon spotted the hotel. Only then did Eileen and I remember that, as were departing our motor coach on arrival, an after-thought occurred to our tour leader. "By the way, the natives refer to this hotel as _____ ." They refused to call it the Radisson, but used its original Hungarian name—probably with great affection.

A dinner cruise on the Danube crowned our stay, but we were to enjoy a longer, more exciting cruise later on in the week. We were happy to leave the next morning for Vienna.

So much has been written about Vienna down through the centuries. What can I possibly say to add to its splendor and beauty! One of our first stops was to visit the Belvedere Palace Gardens, unforgettable brilliant red blossoms laid out in various geometric patterns. They covered the equivalent of several football fields, as we Americans would say. You must see them. The Homburg Winter Palace, near the Vienna city gates, was impressive. I fell in love with St. Stephen's Cathedral, which seemed to dominate the skyline from wherever you were standing. Bathed in light at night, it truly looked as though made of solid gold.

We approached St. Stephen's from a large plaza open to pedestrian traffic only. When we stepped inside this Catholic cathedral, a choir was practicing. A large religious goods shop, in the rear, attracted many tourists, including me. The loveliest souvenir I could possibly buy for myself, I thought, was a silver case for the silver rosary beads I received at my First Communion on May 9, 1929. I hope whichever one of you inherits these treasures will be truly blessed by God.

Nearby, a food court beckoned us. We were thrilled to spot an American chain restaurant. I don't remember whether it was TGIF or Bennigan's, but I remember asking the waitress how come the hamburgers tasted the same as at home. "Oh," she said, "we fly in U.S. beef right from our American headquarters!"

Eileen & Roe Cruising on the Danube

That night we drove to the edge of the Vienna Woods for dinner in one of the traditional wine taverns. Local musicians entertained us with what was called, "Schrammelmusic," and different tourist groups vied with each other in singing their national songs.

Off to Salzburg, via Melk monastery, as mentioned earlier. Some type of religious celebration kept us from visiting the interior, usually open to the public. That was a disappointment for me. On then to the Danube River where we embarked on a large sightseeing cruise ship. This was an absolutely beautiful sail, lasting several hours, along the banks of this famous river. We stopped at several small landings to pick up more passengers. Picturesque churches, cottages, and orchards were scattered along the river banks and up the hillsides. We passed, also, a large castle—Castle Durnstein—which added to the fairyland setting.

Much of what I would say about Salzburg has already been noted in the foregoing e-mail. It was a thrill to stand at the river's edge and look up at the huge castle dominating the hillside. I was thrilled, too, to be in the native city of my very good friends, the von Trapp family. I had heard so much about it for so many years. After a few hours of a walking tour, we returned to the hotel for dinner.

Next morning we were up bright and early to reach Eagle's Nest, Hitler's mountaintop retreat. We were blessed with a remarkably clear view of the surrounding Bavarian Alps. Such a spectacular view of God's magnificent handiwork placed before the eyes of one who brought such devastation and death to millions. Incredible!

We had a long drive back through Bavaria to Germany, and Munich—our destination for the flight home. Our last day, Sunday, was spent at the huge beer hall, earlier described. A fitting end to a beautiful tour of Central Europe.

ENGLAND & SCOTLAND
August 1–13, 2001

Dear Family & Friends,

Here I am again with a write-up of my 5th overseas trip! Can you believe it? After Elaine's wonderful words today about my "writing ability," I'm a little hesitant. Am not sure that I am inspired enough to describe it adequately. It was awesome!

We were a group of forty-four people—all ages. Two over eighty years old (isn't that marvelous - I sill have a future in this escapade!), nine were young people from six to twenty, elementary school to college. We had four family groups, one middle-aged woman with Down's syndrome, more than ten states were represented, and one lovely lady from Auckland, New Zealand. There was the usual percentage of teachers, an administrative assistant from the City of Hartford, Conn., a dentist, a pharmacist, all sizes and shapes of married couples (but no "wife" with handlebar mustache, as on my trip to Ireland!). Our bus driver, Roy, had no sense of humor, couldn't smile, didn't talk or mingle, but, oh, could he whistle. Our tour director, Geraldine, was a walking history book, but loved "our royals" through and through.

Our itinerary on this eleven-day trip started off with arrival in London at 7:00 a.m. Friday, August 2nd, after an overnight flight from Orlando on British Airways. We stayed in London till Sunday. My niece, Eileen, and I were on our own on Friday, and went to Harrod's Dept. Store, and toured downtown by bus.

On Saturday we had a tour to see the "changing of the guard" at Buckingham Palace. We didn't get quite that far—decided to stand in front of Clarendon House, the Queen Mother's home. It was her one hundred-first birthday; we watched and heard the bands, accompanying the guard, play "Happy Birthday" to her. We passed by St. James Palace, the home of Prince Charles; went to St. Paul's Cathedral—the most famous church, after Westminster Abbey—which we never did see.

The Changing of the Guard at Buckingham Palace

Our tour write-up said, if the Queen were in residence at Buckingham Palace, we could not enter, but would visit the summer palace at Balmoral, Scotland, instead. Well, between Sunday and the following Wednesday, when we arrived at Balmoral, the Queen had flown there from London—so we missed out all around. But, skipping ahead to the punch line at the end of this account, if you've seen one castle, you've seen them all.

I knew nothing about Scotland except about "the Tattoo." Scotland is beautiful, especially "the Highlands," and rolling hills filled with sheep on the mountain sides. The mountains look like rocks covered with moss. Few trees. The sheep keep the underbrush, grass, etc. nicely clipped.

Grassmere and Gretna Greene, Scotland, (where a blacksmith is famous for officiating at weddings for couples fleeing across the border from England) were small, uncluttered. Oh, somebody asked me the other day if the countryside was clean. Wow—was it! Not even a beer can, gum wrapper, "Big Gulp," on the roadside. Moving north, the Lake Country was a fairyland. Such beautiful little villages on Lake Windermere—Ambleside for one. We took pictures of Loch Lomond and Lock Ness. Nessie was asleep at the time. The weather was mid-70s throughout all our travels, with occasional light mist.

Our tour group (I couldn't tackle the stairs) toured the Glenlivet Scotch Whiskey Distillery. But I still received my free glass of scotch, plus Eileen's, so I didn't mind a bit. Only in this context is the word "scotch" used. Everything else is "Scottish" as in Scottish people, Scottish tartans, etc. Oh, I fell in love with scones! There are scones and scones, of course, from the biscuit kind with currants (uh-uh) to my favorite little cake, much like a Lorna Doone, but more buttery.

There is so much to cover, so let me condense some of the sightseeing places. We visited Shakespeare's birthplace. The house is exactly the same as it was then, of course, with the exception of the four-lane road, cars, electric heat to keep the tourists warm in fall, etc. Very lovely. Down the road was Anne Hathaway's house where she lived as a girl. Another famous residence—Holyrood, home of Mary, Queen of Scots, when a girl—in Edinburgh. The present-day Queen uses this palace now when on state visits to Scotland.

One of my favorite places was Abbotsford— the home of Sir Walter Scott. Very homey: stone outside, like a castle, but warm, honey-colored wood interior. We stood in his little library where he wrote all his one hundred-fifty poems and thirty-seven plays. Sir Walter was a lawyer who financed a partner in a business venture. It failed, and Walt was left holding the bag. He turned to writing and was able to pay off the millions of dollars debt in three years. Kept on writing after that. The library books from the 1600s and 1700s on are priceless. Beautiful rolling fields, a lovely peacock who made friends. There was a Catholic chapel with pictures of the famous American Cardinal Newman—a friend of the family who visited there, and offered Mass several times. The home is still in habited by Scott's great-great- great granddaughter. (Don't know if I have enough "greats" in there. She is in her 80s.)

Skipping ahead, we went to Belvoir Castle— the home of the Duke and Duchess of Rutland— a young couple with four young children: three little girls aged four, six and eight, and the future Duke, aged two. The natives call it "Beaver Castle." They refuse to acknowledge the French connection of Mary, Queen of Scots. The future Duke was outside to see the bus. It gave us a different feeling to be in a castle where a lively young family lived.

A well-dressed, poised teenager escorted me down the back stairs, since I could no longer climb to the upper floors. He will go to University in another year or two and major in "Heritage Management," combined with Business Management courses. His career goal is to manage these castles, keep them in good repair, make them profitable. Can I go back and start over again? Though, come to think of it, it might be a little stuffy. (Pun intended.)

Back to cities: Glasgow is very industrial, the former site of numerous ship-building companies. Oodles (can't remember statistics at this point of the tour) of huge and famous ocean liners were built there—including the Titanic, and Queen Elizabeth. The latter is now in California.

The Scottish accent here was so think we could not understand a thing anyone said. Our bellhops tried to explain why the plaza in front of the hotel was roped off, with hundreds of police standing by. An illegal Turkish alien was beaten in another section of the country, and died. From what we could make out, through the brogue, there was a trial going on in the courthouse next door and the police were afraid of violence.

Now to Edinburgh - pronounced Edin-bro from "Edwin's Borough" hundreds of years back. Our hotel was situated on "the royal mile"—a one-mile stretch from Holyrood Castle where Mary, Q of S, was born, and grew up to age six. At the other end of the mile is the huge fortress where the Scottish Military Tattoo took place. These performances are held nightly between August 3–25, which accounts for our August trip this time. If I couldn't see it, I didn't want to go!

It was beyond my wildest expectations!. I have never seen, nor expect to see, such an outstanding performance in my lifetime. Maybe in the next. Even though Our Lord has said, "eye has not seen, nor ear heard what great joys await us in heaven," God is going to have to hustle to outshine the Tattoo. Hundreds and hundreds of Scottish regimental troops, each in their own tartans, marched in various formations, while playing bagpipes. Remember, they use both hands on the pipes, while squeezing the air bag under their left arm, keeping in step through intricate marching patterns—all with a swagger of the shoulders (or/and hips) that make those long plaid scarves, flowing from shoulders to ground behind their backs, sway in unison!

The show took an hour and 40 minutes. We had seats just above the entrance/exit, and they all marched right beneath our stand when leaving. Other acts were interspersed. An Irish

Regiment, from Northern Ireland, performed while several dozen young Irish lasses did jigs in unison to the band music. A Polynesian group, in beautiful white costumes, did hula-type dancing, with the Australian Regiment. A young ROTC group showed their expertise in imitating their elders. And how the Russians got involved, I'll never know! They did their very athletic sword dances, men and women with lots of hussahs. And, at times, fireworks went off. And the cannons fired. Did I tell you this was held, at night, in the courtyard of the fort? Awesome!

Nine thousand people attended. The logistics of herding that many people up a steep, wet cobblestone hill, through ONE entrance, is a feat in itself. Hundreds of police asked us to "step forward a few steps please." No whistles, foghorns, guns. "Please put your umbrella down—not permitted." It did not rain during the performance...just during the one-half hour entrance.

I'm writing this part about Edinburgh at 3:30 a.m. I still get so excited about it, I can't sleep, thinking of it all.

We visited York and Yorkminster. "Minster" means "cathedral," so you don't say "Yorkminster Cathedral." The old town was something out of Grimm's Fairy Tales. Very narrow, cobbled streets, with a trough down the middle. That is where the waste was thrown. Butcher Street meant they threw the animal innards and blood out into the street, to flow downhill to the river. Baker Street, likewise, with their waste.

We were told that people didn't bathe in those times. Henry VIII, for example, never had water touch his body in his whole lifetime. That thought made me squirm—you, too? Imagine all the women he slept with? Outside Holyrood, there was a small stone building where Mary,Queen of Scots, bathed twice a year(as we Americans would say—whether she needed it or not). They were afraid of cholera which comes from poor, or no, septic system. These stores from the 1500s are still in use, usually housing trinket shops.

One of these shops is now a Shrine to St. Margaret Clitherow. She was a butcher's wife; in 1571 she married at age fifteen, a Catholic convert, mother of several children. Scotland went from Catholic to Protestant, back to Catholic, depending who was on the throne. Margaret smuggled priests into her town; Masses were offered in secret hiding places. She was put in prison because she would not reveal the names of the priests, fearing they would be killed. She was laid on a slab of wood, with a door on top of her, like a sandwich. They kept putting heavy boulders on top of her, literally pressing her to death. She was declared a saint in 1970.

Our last stop, before returning to London, was at Cambridge and the University. A very *busy place with thousands of tourists. The University was not in regular session. As you know, Europe shuts down for the month of August since workers are given a month's vacation all at the same time. The tourists take over, which delights hoteliers and shopkeepers. Only in Florence were all the shops closed when we were there. Cambridge was really the only place where we saw elite shops and high priced clothing: tweeds, tartans, etc. (A tartan, complete outfit, starts at about $1,000.) Perhaps our tour avoided these places, though that is unusual. We visited lots of tea rooms and trinket shops at noon time. Must mention "the mathematical bridge," built by a young Cambridge student, hundreds of years ago, without nails, screws etc. Years later, engineers took it apart, trying to duplicate the feat, and they couldn't. Put it back together with brackets, nails...*

Cheryl and I at London Bridge, Christmas Time

My last night included dinner at a fine Italian restaurant in London—the best meal we had—followed by a cruise along the Thames to see Parliament, and all the government buildings, lit up. Very impressive, especially sailing under the London Tower Bridge, not like freezing December temps in fog and rain on my last visit.

It's 4:50 a.m.; I'm getting hungry, and this is getting long-winded. Any questions, e-mail me and I'll share the answers with the rest of the gang.

To sum up (and I bet you all peeked to see the punch line!): our friendly bus driver who took us to Gatwick Airport, London at 6:30 a.m. on our departure, asked one of our group where we had gone. Joe, our amiable resident dentist, told him.

"Oh, another ABC tour," the bus driver said.

"What is an ABC tour?" asked Joe.

"Another Bloody Castle!"

Love to each and every one...."

August 26, 2001

ENGLAND & SCOTLAND
August 1 - 12, 2001

LONDON
December 3 - 10, 1999

Did you notice I hinted several times about an earlier visit to London? That happened in December, 1999, when my nephew Jerry invited me to accompany him and daughter, Cheryl, as their guest for a week's stay. I had three days to prepare for take-off, and on return got so caught up in Christmas activities that I did not record the event. I am tucking some of our doings into this narrative.

There was a huge difference between these two trips. December was bitterly cold. I have never been so cold in my life, even though the temperature averaged twenty-nine degrees above zero. It was very damp, with a chilling wind that gnawed at one's bones. Dressed in black pants, black London Fog coat over layers of clothing, white Reeboks and white hood and scarf, I was no fashion plate. White shoes quickly labeled me as an American. Everyone was dressed totally in black - no color on any passerby. Unlike many caricatures of British statesmen, never saw an umbrella either.

Cheryl was accompanied by her two sons, aged about five and twelve. Being an overseas flight attendant for U. S Airlines, Cheryl was very familiar with London because of her many layovers there. She must have used her free time wisely, as she very competently guided us on the subway and bus systems. We stayed in an apartment hotel, complete with kitchen and upstairs loft. Every day we were out and about to see new things, despite the cold.

A thrilling highlight for me was a visit to the world-renowned Harrod's Department Store. It was so beautifully decorated for Christmas, both inside and outside. The toy department was a virtual treasure—several floors with large rooms each devoted to dolls, or perhaps stuffed animals, or trains. The rich and famous from all over the word shop there for toys found nowhere else—life-sized, or one-of-a-kind, or opulently decked out.

I had bragged about all this to Eileen and, of course, it was the first place we headed for upon my return to London nineteen months later. What a let down! The toy department in summer had shrunk in size to part of one floor. Where a whole room, at Christmas time, was filled with a certain item, it was now located on just at a few shelves in a far-off corner. We could have been in any Fifth Avenue store in New York City.

The Tower of London was not the skyscraper I expected; and I did not know the Royal Crown Jewels were on display there. That was awesome. They were encased in huge glass cabinets and, of course, well guarded. Right outside is the famous London Tower Bridge. Very square, short, medieval looking. I was impressed, but seeing it at night, all lit up, while cruising down the Thames in August, really put the icing on the cake.

We visited Madame Tussaud's Wax Museum, quite different from the famous wax museum in Montreal. Here, in

London, at the original Madame Tussaud's, the figures were not housed in glass cages. Rather, you might enter a large salon and see groups of men standing about, perhaps chatting with ladies seated on satin-covered chairs. They were so life-like. Or you might walk down a hallway and almost be tempted to nod to the Queen or ask Pope John Paul II for at a blessing. We spent many interesting hours there.

One night Cheryl said we were going to see *Cats*, the longest-running musical in both London's West End, and on Broadway. I was not turned on. Not a lover of cats. How could anyone portray them? I ate my words! It was the most fascinating live performance I have ever witnessed. All actors were dressed up as cats. They slithered along the floor like cats. They snarled, climbed, chased each other. And there was at a good story line, with excellent music and singing. I was super-fascinated.

I cannot say much about restaurants, since we dined out only once on our first night in London, as guests of five-year old Asher's Dad, Larry, an airline pilot. This was in the famous Soho district. At ten o'clock at night the three-story restaurant was packed. The food was great - but what I remember most was that Asher loved snails and ate two platefuls of them. Quite an unusual taste for a child.

We grabbed lunch each day at little tea rooms or tiny counters around town. I quickly learned that any tuna sandwich in London had corn kernels in the mix! At night the Lamour clan ate in our apartment, after a wearisome and footsore day. Pizza, cheese-crackers-wine, fresh fruit gave us strength to face the next sightseeing day.

I attended Sunday Mass, and that of the feast day, December 8th (Immaculate Conception of Mary) at a Redemptorist Church a few blocks from our hotel. Was I surprised that the

Mass was the way I remembered it as at a child, with the priest having his back to the people and the responses in Latin. I expected the English to be more avant-garde than that. The childrens' choir was heavenly.

On my second trip to London and beyond, Eileen and I were fortunately able to fly out of Orlando, directly to London. My letter to family and friends was quite inclusive as to our activities, so I will only highlight here some that were overlooked. That would include the ferry to the Isle of Skye, which serves as a connector between England and Scotland. This ferry was huge. It was quite a shock to see the whole bow rise straight up into the air, upon docking, to reveal a large number of cars waiting to depart. Eileen's excitement was that Princess Anne almost bumped into her. The Princess was late getting to the dock, but was quickly whisked up to the bridge upon arrival.

Scotland is a very relaxing place. The mountains are low, stretching out in long chains as far as the eye can see. The grass is clipped short by the herds of animals roaming free, and picturesque small towns appear from time to time. A lovely scene I will always remember was a small Scottish tearoom where locals stopped in for tea, lugging their canvas shopping bags with them. Scones of all sizes and shapes were amply displayed. We were in the lake country, approaching Lochs Lomond and Ness and Windemere. I could have stayed forever.

While we were unable to visit the Castle at Balmoral, we did visit the centuries-old Crathie Church where the "royals" worship when in residence in Scotland.

On to St. Andrews from there. What a shock. While I don't know anything about golf, I understand that St. Andrews is the holy mecca of that sport. I pictured rolling, sculptured hills, ponds, little foot bridges—the amenities of our best courses here at home. St. Andrews was as flat as a pancake; it looked like a football field. A white railing surrounding it also put you in mind of a race track. Another surprise, it was situated right on the edge of a rough, tumbling sea—windy, and filled with white caps, while we were there. St. Andrews University was across the road. It did not seem to have much of a campus—rather small stone houses and buildings laid out on city streets. We stopped into a small pub in one of these brownstones for a wee nip to take the chill off.

Back to London again, Eileen and I split up to take trips separately. She wanted to see the Tower of London. I had seen it, so chose a cruise on the Thames. When she took a return trip to Harrod's, I found visiting with part of our group in the hotel's pub a pleasant way to spend a couple of hours. This trip seemed to come quickly to an end. England and Scotland were never on my wish list. Now I know what I would have missed.

My concluding words of wisdom: there are marvelous things to see and do, wherever you find yourself. Go for it!

ALASKA
July 27–August 3, 2003

Dear Friends & Family—

"Sailing, sailing over the bounding main...."
We were "sailing" so well that, with no one in
the swimming pool on the top deck of the
Volendam, there were waves. Water was
splashing from one side to the other. That is
how my stomach felt. Everyone says, "don't
worry about a thing, they have stabilizers
now." Well, the sea-sickness carried over to the
seven-day land portion of our trip as well.

The Volendam was a beautiful ship of the
Holland-American Line. We were next to the
lowest deck, mid-ship (my request) and our
cabins were terrific. I wanted to take my bed
home with me. We maneuvered to get first
seating at dinner, and Robertus fell all over us
with service and graciousness. The dinners (all
the food) were delicious. Breakfast and lunch
were cafeteria style, with a food bar that
seemed to wind half-way around the deck.

Other than part of the ship's crew putting on a variety show, there were no other activities. You made your own. Hang out in one of the multiple bars and watch the mountains and sea go by, or swim, or visit the casino. This is very foreign to Floridians' idea of a cruise: big bands, buffet at midnight under the stars, dancing, etc. People here thought I was joking. It was a very staid, middle-aged group, with only one baby and maybe three or four children.

We had daily Mass. The "chaplain of the week" was a Father Frank from Albion, Nebraska. He used his week as a retreat. Holland-American advertises that there is a chaplain aboard every sailing. Father Frank had a great sense of humor with stories about being a farm boy, and now a priest in farm country. He asked me to lector the first day and, when I got up on the stage, that is when I started to sway. And swayed, and dizzied through the next ten days. Narrow gauge railroads, and old school buses to get up the narrow, winding, gravel roads towards Mt. McKinley, did nothing for me. I sat out three events and don't even remember White Horse.

Eileen and I wished we had stayed on the ship for a week. Then we might have seen an iceberg! The biggie I really wanted to experience! Don't know if there is any guarantee anyway. Only two cruise ships a day are allowed into Glacier Bay. Everywhere we went, there were four or five cruise liners, either at the piers, or parked, waiting to get in. Wonder if it was a lottery which ships would see the glaciers?

We disembarked at Skagway, Canada, a town of 850 permanent residents and 10,000 sightseers, when all the cruise ships pull in the same morning! The town was three streets long and two streets in depth, either side. From there we took the White Pass & Yukon Railroad, a narrow-gauge railroad built at the turn of the twentieth century in an effort to help with the Klondike Gold Rush of 1898. Though men worked long hard hours throughout grueling winters, sleeping in makeshift accommodations next to the tracks, it was completed just as the Gold Rush fizzled out only two years later.

We hooked up with our Holland-American motor coach driven by Colman, a twenty-three-year-old Mormon student studying dentistry, and a younger tour leader, Paul, a P. E. major in British Columbia, but a native of Anchorage. They enjoyed little jokes, like telling us one rural hotel was out of toilet paper. They passed around a roll of tissue, and we all entered the lobby with a wad of paper in each hand. This happened at Beaver Creek, "301 miles from nowhere" as the dining staff sang to us at dinner. It was an old Army site, and we slept in beautifully reconditioned barracks, without telephone and TV. No doubt, AC too—we didn't need to explore that one.

The weather was ideal, temperature-wise; in 70s during the day. They said it was in the 40s at night, but we were so comfy in each hotel, we did not know. We never saw a bug, despite others' testimony. I left a quart of insect spray at the Marriott in Anchorage for the chambermaid. You just can't believe campers! I would not want to camp there anyway—miles and miles from nowhere if you break down. Crude-looking campgrounds at the roadside. I never did see a well-kept residential area. The bus driver said there was a big contest to see who could spend the least money on the ugliest home in Alaska. We saw four hours of sun. It is a rainy, misty, dreary atmosphere. Mental depression is a major disease here.

We visited a fish hatchery, the Mendenhall Glacier, a gold mine, and a trip around Fairbanks by boat (missed these two trips), an eight-hour bus ride by school bus up the steep mountainside to get within forty-six miles of Mt. McKinley. I bailed out of that one after ninety minutes. The bus driver gave me a clear (see through) thirty-three gallon garbage bag to throw up in, as he dropped me off at a rest stop. I hitch-hiked back to the hotel on two other buses in order to reach the Denali Park Inn.

Alaska - View from Fairbanks-Anchorage Train

College kids (and teachers) are the backbone of the tourist industry in the Yukon-Klondike and Alaska areas. Everything shuts up tight on September 18th when the cruise ships stop running. By then, the natives expect snow and are holing up for the winter. I met a bus driver who goes fifty miles inland from the Denali Forest to live in a self-built log cabin, with his wife, for the winter, plus twelve huskies, two sleds, and no electronic communication. They had a busy winter last year; two snowmobilers found them.

We stopped at a place called "Riga's," named after a forty year old European woman who migrated to Alaska to live out her life. At eighty-seven, a Christmas fire totaled her little cabin (she dove through the window). She supported and cared for herself until ninety-seven. Today a religious group leases the restored, pioneer settlement, from the government, since the state cannot afford to staff it. Much like Williamsburg, there are log buildings housing shops for smithys, carpenters, weavers, etc. And the best rhubarb-strawberry pie in the world, Colman and Paul said. We then knew why they did not eat at our 10:30 a.m. "lunch stop" which was a Holland-American hotel.

Holland-American owned the railroad cars, many of the sight-seeing venues, as well as five of the Westmark Hotels at which we stayed. That is why every hotel had the same dinner menu, offering five entrees from about $24 - $27. (A hamburger was $10.) Eileen and I had free $250 meal vouchers for the seven-day land trip. (Free, because our travel agent bargained for them.) Even if you had to pay for the vouchers, it would have been a deal.

We ended our trip with a scheduled eight hour (turned out as nine and a half hours) train ride on a beautiful Holland-American train from Fairbanks, south to Anchorage. The roof was a complete glass dome. There was a bar on the upper level, where we sat, the dining room was on the floor beneath us. In the "basement" was the luggage. "Bar" was for anything liquid

- milk, coffee, hot chocolate, martini, etc. We started off with the tour director telling us all about the splendid features of this newly designed car, and only one drawback: "It sways more than any other car on the line." Funny enough, I made out quite well.

Then, for me, it was a ten hour overnight flight from Anchorage to Newark, Newark to Orlando, and a sixty mile drive home in my car. About one hour out from Orlando on the plane, I developed "kennel cough"—the best way to describe the wheezing. It escalated quickly. My doctor diagnosed a viral infection. I am on a ten-day regimen of medications to combat it. Yesterday and today I am beginning to feel like me.

"Alaska—the Last Frontier" is not without rich meaning. Certainly the people are hardy, proud of their accomplishments and those of their ancestors. Rightly so. Would I make this trip again? You just cannot go from fifty years of ties with Vermont to see someone else's trees, and think they are better! After the first ten thousand Alaskan trees, the next million are not so exciting.

I think, too, that our Vermont mountains are more huggable!

Love to all,

August 17, 2003

Juneau, Alaska Harbor

ALASKA
July 27–August 3, 2003

Amen!

I can think of nothing to add to the foregoing letter I sent to your families upon my return from Alaska. This was the forty-ninth state I have visited. The phrase, "from sea to shining sea" means so much to me. I wish all of you the opportunity to follow in my footsteps and form your own assessments of what riches this country has, both in its natural resources and its people.

Happy traveling!

My love to you all—

MEME

P.S. I will let you guess which is the fiftieth, and last, state I have yet to see. While I said last year that, after Alaska, my traveling days were over, I just could not resist the Queen Mary 2. Yet, if I decide I just have to attend a hot air balloon convention some day, don't be surprised to find a new last, last chapter!

QUEEN MARY 2
Caribbean Cruise: March 6–16, 2004

Dear Family & Friends,

To tell you about my ten-day Caribbean trip on the Queen Mary 2 confines me to talking about the ship itself. It was the ultimate cruise! It tried to offer all things to all shipmates aboard: fine dining, up-scale shopping, casino, high-end body pampering in the spa, daily art auctions of the works of fine masters worth $5,000,000, operatic entertainment in the evening, a planetarium (where Mass was celebrated daily), many cocktail lounges, a library, and enough food to feed an army— which they did. It was announced that 10,000 meals were served daily. I thought it would be a higher number since we were over 2,600 passengers, and a crew ratio of one staff to each two passengers. Guess some people did not eat breakfast.

Queen Mary 2

Not to be overlooked were complete (free) laundromats on the cabin decks, and the swimming pools. Guests on the upper floors, and in the upper financial curve, had their own restaurants and grills, kennel, nannies and butlers. In this category, grand duplex apartments were $23,000 to $26,000. The Penthouse was a mere $10,949. Eileen and I were in the middle price range for cabins at $2,429 each, with a "premium balcony." A higher price scale will be in effect for the regularly scheduled transatlantic crossings to start soon after our cruise was finished.

To put all this into its nautical setting, let me insert the ship's statistics:
Length: 1132 feet
Width: 135 feet.
At the Bridge Wings: width is 147.5 feet

Draft: *32 feet, 10 inches*
Height: *236.2 feet from keel to funnel*
Tonnage: *150,000 gross tons appx.*
Passengers: 2,650
Crew: *1,253*
Speed: *30 knots approx. 34.5 mph*
Power: *157,000 horsepower—gas turbine/diesel electric plant*
Propulsion:4 pods of 21.5 MW each—2 fixed and 2 azimuthing*
Extra thick hull for strength and stability for Atlantic Crossings.
2 stabilizers
 # decks: *14*
Cost: *$800,000,000*

* It can turn completely around within its own length, and does not require docking assistance from tugs.

Eileen and I were on deck #4 in a very comfortable stateroom. The king-size bed was divided into single beds. We enjoyed a small refrigerator, safe, computer, a TV with remote that offered many electronic capabilities, bath with shower, loads of closet space, sitting area with sofa. Sliding glass doors opened out onto our private balcony with lounge chairs and a small table. Phone, hair dryer, bathrobe and slippers were provided. A bottle of champagne awaited us on arrival—compliments of the captain.

Never has it been so easy to gain access to any activity or facility...or to spend money! Each of us was issued a guest card, resembling a credit card. Whether you were charging a drink, playing bingo, opening your cabin door, purchasing a $130 Queen Mary 2 sweatshirt, or visiting the medical facility, the only thing required was your "Queen Mary 2 Passenger Card." Even tipping the wait staff and chamber maid was made easy by the pursers adding $121 to each bill—rated at $11/day. Our shore excursions were incorporated into this charging system. The only exception seemed to be in the lounges. The drink price was listed - e.g. Martini $4.75; beneath it a gratuity of perhaps 25%; then a subtotal and a line for "tip." It only took one or two drinks to catch on that we were double tipping. The final "final total" then went to the purser and our account. But the drinks were good!

Because of the length of the ship, there was much walking. When we stepped outside our cabin door amid-ship, we looked up and down the hall, in either direction, into infinity. There were four banks of elevators and stairs. One had to know which set of elevators, A - B - C - D, you needed. There were almost no directional signs. I would have settled for "port" and "starboard' as all the even-numbered rooms were on one side of the ship, and the odd numbers on the other. Since there were no windows at hand in the elevator areas, I couldn't tell if I was walking fore or aft.

The motion of the ship was remarkably absent. Eileen and I felt vibration when lying in bed at night—one night I got up several times to silence the clothes hangars. It seemed to us that this vibration occurred every other night. We wondered if they alternated the ship's engines. Nevertheless, I always wore my wrist bands designed to mitigate motion sickness. Perhaps the most vibration was felt down on deck #2 at Mass in the Planetarium. The back of the huge hall was reached on deck #3, the stage area at the bottom of the sloping aisles was on deck #2.

I felt privileged to be the lector (scripture reader) at Mass each day during our ten-day trip. Missed one day because our shore trip was scheduled for 8:00 a.m. (which finally took off after 9:00 a.m.). Monsignor McClain, our cruise chaplain from Iowa, had us sit through one Mass because of the swaying, and he kept a chair right next to him in case he could not stand upright either. The auditorium sat 500 people and it was almost completely filled for the two Sunday Masses. God is upon the sea.

Did you catch the scheduling delay just above? This was almost endemic to such a huge ship with so many passengers. There were always long lines for everything, from a seat at the buffet lunch, to getting a cocktail at 6:00 p.m., to boarding and disembarking. When we reached Ft. Lauderdale, Fl. by motor coach at 12:30 p.m. on March 6th to begin our voyage, we immediately found ourselves in lines, four to six people across. From outside the terminal, we shuffled inside to repeat the process again, as we went through metal detectors. Then we entered a huge upstairs floor that resembled a warehouse. Computers lined one wall, but they went "down" for forty-five minutes. We sat where we could. Elite passengers went right through a separate bank of machines and inspectors. It was not until 3:30 p.m. that we boarded Queen Mary 2.

Included in our travel package was one dinner at the very posh Todd English Restaurant—by reservation only. Two days before embarking, the Cunard Line decided to levy a charge of $30 per person for this epicurean delight. Despite much uproar, Cunard stood by its guns. Our tour leader suggested that, in rebuttal, we ask the purser to deduct the $30 from the $121 tipping fee they were charging us. Some of us felt, however, that we were only harming the over-burdened staff.

Our chambermaid, Letzminda, arrived at 7:00 a.m., and was still on our floor distributing the ship's paper, turning down beds, and leaving the well-touted piece of chocolate after 9:00 p.m. the same day. One of the cocktail waitresses told us she worked from 11:00 a.m. to 2:00 p.m. in one of the lounges, off-duty two hours, then worked from 4:00 p.m. to 2:00 a.m. the next morning—shifting around to the various cocktail areas on board, as needed. We saw the "bingo crew" in all sorts of posts, from assisting in the disembarking onto tenders, to helping photographers.

The ship's photographers were everywhere, starting with our struggle to board in Ft. Lauderdale. The line of passengers was held up while each couple was stopped in its tracks to be photographed. Photographers were gathered outside the lounges and restaurants in the evening, especially enticing those in formal dress to pose and smile for the occasion. A huge display of these pictures was set up on one of the lower decks and ship's crew stood by to accept your order.

Four formal evenings were announced. I guess this rubbed some guests the wrong way since each day we were reminded that the day's dress code would be enforced—especially at the entrance to the Britannia Restaurant. I believe one such night was canceled. Eileen and I wore evening skirts on only two nights, and on a third night we escaped to the lunch buffet area which was converted into four specialty dining areas: Italian, Asian, British, and "watch the chef." We found our Italian meal to be the best served, tastiest, quietest, and most efficient dinner during the ten days. Of course, we must not overlook room service which we settled for one night. Within a half hour we had a great pizza. That was a noteworthy feat!

Britannia Restaurant, Queen Mary 2

Dinner in the evening was reserved seating in a particular restaurant, determined by the price of one's ticket. We were assigned, along with two thousand of our closest friends, to the Britannia Restaurant. There were two seatings— our group was chosen for the earlier seating at 6:00 p.m. Eileen and I sat with six other tour members. The table behind us was also a group of eight from Melbourne, Fl. The rest of our party, another fifteen or so, were seated on the opposite side of the huge restaurant. You could say the opposite side of the ship. The room was that large. We didn't get to know the other half until our tour guide leaders threw a cocktail party for the whole group two nights before our return to Florida.

Seated at our table was a ninety-year-old gentleman and his wife. Charlie was very knowledgeable about the space program, NASA, etc. It would not have surprised me if he were an official of one of these agencies at some time in his life. Charlie loved chocolate ice cream with chocolate sauce, and asked for it every night, even though it was not on the menu. Needless to say, I would order, "same as Charlie," so we hit it off just fine. His daughter, Marie and her friend, Aretha, were from Atlanta. I understand Marie is, or was, a psychiatrist. These two ladies were lots of fun— they didn't miss a night at the casino, nor much of anything else. Don, a former Army officer in Vietnam, sat with his wife opposite Eileen and me. Since Eileen's dad was an Army colonel, they found lots of topics to talk about. Dining was really a very pleasant part of the day.

Menus changed daily—not like Alaska! Soup and salad courses were offered before the entree. Cannot speak for the soup, but I enjoyed the salads. Entrees were very small, but exquisitely "presented," as chefs would say. While we never had a serving of vegetables as such, slivers of green beans or carrots might decorate the plate. The meats were usually disguised in some way—not a simple slice of chicken. The best meal of all was three small lobster tails, already split, and "fork ready." Desserts were cremes, an occasional pie or tart. Nothing was spicy. The word we used in England so often, "bland," fits well here also. Service was extremely slow; dinner was at least a two-hour event.

We got to know the ship very well. Only four times did we disembark for shore trips. Our tour director chose the most comprehensive trip around each island, which gave us a great scenic overview. These trips were about two to three hours in length, ending up back at port side in the midst of huge flea markets selling all kinds of souvenirs. The method of transportation was usually a bus of some sort. On one memorable occasion, in St. Maarten, we were perched on benches which seemed to be bolted down to a pick-up. It had an awning stretched out overhead to protect us from the sun—or rain.

Swimming Pools, Queen Mary 2

Our driver, on this particular day, was very vocal and informative. He was especially excited about a new building half-way up the mountain, in a poor neighborhood of shacks. Our driver said there had been much fighting about it. Unlike other bus drivers, he would take us around to the front of the building. Going around a sharp, hill-hugging curve, he pulled up so we could take pictures of : Dee Home Dee-POT. All twenty passengers were in hysterics. He must have thought he had the only "Home Dee-POT" in the world!

On our first day ashore, we went to the Gatun Locks of the Panama Canal. It was most interesting to see a huge freighter come through a lock. It was so low you could only see the mast and wheel house. Water flowed in by gravity and the ship rose quickly in front of our eyes so we were looking skyward to see the portholes. Then a big gate opened sideways and let the freighter through to the next set of locks. I understand it takes eight to nine hours to make the whole passage from Atlantic to Pacific oceans. The Queen Mary 2, and other large cruise ships, are too big to enter at all. Panama is planning to dig a parallel canal that could accommodate them.

Eileen was appalled at the poverty evident in Panama. We judged unemployment was high, due to the many groups of men hanging around on street corners; houses and shacks were in states of disrepair. One wonders if the population was not better off when five U. S. Military installations oversaw the safety and operation of the locks. While the posts were self-sufficient, the native citizenry benefitted from the American dollars brought into their midst.

Roe at Gatun Locks, Panama

It took ten years to build the Panama Canal: 1904-1914. In 1914 the Isthmian Canal Commission was abolished, and replaced by a permanent administrative entity, operating in conjunction with the Panama Railroad Company. Restructuring of this organization took place in 1951 and 1979. The Panama

Canal Commission took over the operation of the waterway in '79. The Republic of Panama assumed territorial jurisdiction of the former Canal Zone and Panamanian laws went into force in the area. On December 31, 1999, Panama assumed full responsibility for the administration, operation and maintenance of the Panama Canal. The U. S. bases were closed.

Our next port-of-call was to have been Cartagena, Colombia. In mid-December, I received a Travel Warning from the U. S. Dept. of State. It read:

"The Department of State warns U.S. Citizens against travel to Colombia. Violence by narco-terrorist groups and other criminal elements continues to affect all parts of the country, urban and rural. Citizens of the United States and other countries continue to be the victims of threats, kidnappings, and other violence. This threat has increased recently in urban areas, including, but not limited to Bogota, Cartagena and Barraquilla... Bombings have caused civilian casualties throughout Colombia. Targets include supermarkets, places of entertainment, and other areas where U.S. citizens congregate."

After we set sail, the Cunard Line announced we would by-pass Colombia and have more time in Curacao.

Our stop in Willemstad, Curacao, made local history. We docked parallel to the shore at a new, huge cement pier specially built to accommodate the Queen Mary 2. School children in plaid uniforms, with white shirts, marched down to the beautifully landscaped park beside the beach. At supper time, hundreds of cars lined up on shore. When we sailed at midnight, fireworks sent us on our way. It was the first time such a huge ship had stopped to visit.

While I had come down with a bad cough and was treated by the medical facility that morning, it seemed best for me to stay aboard. Nevertheless, I enjoyed lounging in a deck chair, looking out to the beautiful harbor, the three and four-story buildings painted in vivid blue, green, coral and yellow. A canal nearby swallowed up huge freighters as they headed into port. It was always so exciting for me to see other large cruise ships and freighters appear on the horizon out of nowhere. Many passed quite close; perhaps they too wanted to see the largest cruise ship in the world!

Our last stop was at Charlotte Amalie, St. Thomas, in the U.S. Virgin Islands. Immediately, one had the feeling we were in our own country. Everything was much tidier and neater and cleaner. Of course, having a huge American hotel, the former Blue Beard Castle (a tourist site), greeting us at the entrance to the bay, emphasized this feeling. St. Thomas vistas from the hill tops were the most beautiful we had seen. We missed a huge rainstorm while we were bussing up to the highest peak. Down below, the town was all puddle-y and wet when we returned. It is a place I would like to revisit.

What were the pluses and minuses of this trip for me personally? Three surprises were immediately apparent—the number of elderly, handicapped guests aboard. Every sort of walker, electric cart, crutches and braces were evident. It is so great that handicapped people are able to travel with ease... and are welcome, as well.

The opposite side of the coin—I don't believe there were more than ten or twelve children aboard. Outside of accompanying their parents to the pool, there was little for them to do. I wonder if the days didn't drag for both parents and their offspring. There was a nursery with a few cribs and nanny to attend to babies, while their parents dined in the upper class restaurants.

If a coin can have three sides, the large group of gay men on board was overwhelming at first. They cruised around in groups of six to eight usually, were very well-groomed and well-dressed. They looked like junior, if not senior, executives. I sat with several of these men at lunch and was delightfully surprised to find an old-fashioned politeness and courtesy to each other and those around them. One gentleman had been an art teacher at Melbourne High school at the same time I was professionally involved with the guidance counselors there.

I certainly would include the stately and picturesque metallic works of art that reached from floor to ceiling in open hallways and staircases. The beautiful and numerous crystal chandeliers were monumental. Rich, dark wood paneling in the lounges and dining room were elegant.

Twice the Queen Mary 2 was unable to dock at ports-of-call because of her immense size. Then we boarded tenders which took us from the ship, out in the bay, to land. These tenders, motorized life boats, sat one hundred people, were furnished with life jackets for each passenger. A crew of three helped us aboard. They were so adept at handling people safely and comfortably from the steady liner, onto the bouncing tender fighting the seas. A pilot ran the engines. His head stuck up through a sunroof, where he could also watch some of the passengers sitting up on the roof. Most exciting part of the trip!

These are my pluses.

Disappointments: a ten-day cruise was really too long for me. Seven days would have suited me better. We left Ft. Lauderdale on a Saturday, and it was Tuesday before we left the ship for a shore excursion. On the return, we set sail for home on Sunday afternoon and disembarked in Florida on Tuesday. I do enjoy the sea very much, but the crowds and confinement on board ship were beginning to pall.

The nightly entertainment was not what I expected. Rather than two or three nights of opera, a juggler, the planetarium, etc., I had expected first-run movies (there was a year-old horror movie the first night), perhaps a concert, big-name personalities and performers, and the like. I was really disappointed that native talent from the islands we were visiting were not invited aboard to put on a show. That really would have highlighted the cultures we met each day.

Eileen and I were not very resourceful, perhaps, in digging out lesser-known activities. One lady told me how busy she been, taking painting lessons. I hesitate to think what the cost would have been. There were some exotic trips on shore: helicopter rides over the canal, canoe trips, a sail on board a schooner, snorkeling, etc. that were big-buck items. Eileen dragged me to afternoon bingo twice. $20 was the minimum purchase. The second time we went, it was one game for the $20. The jackpot was $1600, which one of our group won.

I am glad I sailed aboard the Queen Mary 2. The anticipation was more of a thrill than the actuality...but isn't that usually the case.

The word "awesome" is often over-worked, but—standing alone at a ship's railing, looking out to the horizon, with no visible sign of men or ships, watching the swells and white caps—that is awesome. How mighty is the Creator who made the sunrise and sunset, the moon beams tracing a path on the waves; it takes one's breath away. We will stand before Him all alone one day, face to face...and that will be more awesome.

I was reminded of two of my favorite bible stories: Jesus walking on the water, and also the time He fell asleep in a fishing boat while a storm raged all around Him. Just think how many men and ships have sailed the mighty oceans ever since.

I often thought of the Titanic as I strolled through Queen Mary 2's famous rotunda, or climbed the grand staircase, or studied the fantastic decor - how all of this same grandeur, decades ago, merely slipped into the sea.

The next time I hear the "Navy Hymn," I will remember all these things, and will be even more mindful of "those in peril on the sea."

Printed in the United Kingdom
by Lightning Source UK Ltd.
125071UK00001B/46/A